The Man Who Built a City

By Rosemary Weir

THE STAR AND THE FLAME

HIGH COURAGE

THE LION AND THE ROSE

THE MAN WHO BUILT A CITY

The Man Who Built a City

A LIFE OF SIR CHRISTOPHER WREN

by

ROSEMARY WEIR

An Ariel Book
Farrar, Straus & Giroux
New York

First edition, 1971

Library of Congress catalog card number 74-161371
ISBN 0-374-35008-6

Published simultaneously in Canada
by Doubleday Canada Ltd., Toronto

Printed in the United States of America

Designed by Sheila Lynch

Author's Note

NOT VERY MUCH is known about the private life of Sir Christopher Wren. He did not keep a diary, as did his friends Samuel Pepys and Sir John Evelyn. He wrote very few letters. Moreover, he was a reserved man; he did not give away his secret thoughts and feelings to his friends, so when they write of him they tell us only of his achievements, not of his hopes and fears.

And yet, in spite of this, a portrait emerges, the portrait of a kind man, a tolerant man, never touchy and difficult, always calm and polite. To those who were not close friends he may have seemed remote, for his mind was engaged in a constant battle to find truth, the truth of scientific principles, the truth about the stars, the human body, and a hundred and one other things.

Wren was a practical man. He loved to use his hands, to make models, and to conduct experiments. He seems to have been disinterested in the arts, except the art of building, and this is strange, for in his time most gentlemen of education took an active interest in music, painting, and sculpture. Pepys and his friends "made music" all night through; Sir John Evelyn was a patron of the arts. It was he who befriended Grinling Gibbons the carver and brought his work to the attention of the King. But Wren seems to have stood aside from all that and only interested himself in art when it touched his own field of endeavor. Music to him meant little more than the right placing of an organ in a church. Paintings were something that was necessary to cover the ceiling and walls; wood and stone carving was embroidery on the fabric of his buildings.

In trying to trace the life of this indomitable man, I have read many books and have found that the accounts given in them sometimes contradict one another. I have had to select what I consider the most likely, and in this I have been helped by the fact that "Kit" Wren has become so real to me that I sometimes feel I know him as one knows an intimate friend. Now that my book is finished, I leave him as sadly as if he had indeed been my friend. My hope is that you who read what I have written will feel the same.

R. W.

Contents

Part IV
A TIME OF ACHIEVEMENT

Part V
THE DECLINING YEARS

The Man Who Built a City

The modest man built the city and the modest man's skill was unknown. But surely posterity are obliged to allow him that praise after death, which he so industriously declined while he was living.

The Tatler

Introduction

WHEN, in all the towns and villages of England, the church bells rang in the first year of the seventeenth century they rang in an era of swifter and greater changes than, perhaps, England had ever known. Before the century was over, the population was called upon to endure plague, fire, and the horrors of civil war, which tore the country apart, setting brother against brother and father against son. A reigning monarch lost his life barbarously on the block, at the hands of his own subjects. Fierce battles were fought at sea against the Dutch.

An era of trouble, and yet at the same time an era that produced forward-looking men who took giant strides in the realms of basic knowledge, who began to rid themselves of the superstitions of the past, and who worked eagerly and unceasingly to find the truth. They explored the little-understood worlds of astronomy, mathematics, and medical science. They were endlessly inventive and wonderfully creative. Many of these men were born during the first half of the century, and among them was a tiny, delicate, precocious child whose name was Christopher Wren. He grew up to be a man outstanding even among his brilliant colleagues, for not only was he gifted with an exceptional brain and an insatiable thirst for knowledge, not only was he a man of vision, but he was also a practical man, who, when he turned his genius to building, had the power to transmute his dreams into enduring reality, for men to use, admire, and enjoy.

Wren is chiefly remembered today as the man who rebuilt St. Paul's Cathedral after the Great Fire of London in 1666. He is the only man who undertook the building of a cathedral and lived to see it completed. It took thirty-five years, a large slice of any man's working life, and yet St. Paul's is only a part of the long success story that is Christopher Wren's. He lived just under ninety-one years, and from early childhood until a short time before his quiet death he invented, explored, probed, planned—sharpening his wits against the wits of his friends, using his skill to put into tangible shape the visions of his brain.

Sir Christopher Wren was a man of his time, but his work lives on to enrich our own time and time yet to come.

Part I

THE MIRACLE YOUTH

That prodigious young scholar . . .
SIR JOHN EVELYN

1

Early Days

THE TWENTIETH OF OCTOBER in the year 1632 was a happy day for the rector of East Knoyle, Wiltshire, a county in the south of England. It was a day for which he and his wife had anxiously waited, the day upon which his second son was born. There had been another son the year before, but he had died at birth, a great grief to a man who so far had only daughters. They were good little girls and he loved them dearly, but daughters are their mother's concern and a man longs for a son to fashion after himself and to carry on his name. Dr. Christopher Wren, rector of St. Mary's Church, for the second time baptized a little boy Christopher and prayed that this one might live to manhood, for in those days infant mortality was shockingly high.

The new Christopher was a delicate, undersized child, but although for a time it seemed as if he would follow his brother into the grave, he managed to struggle through babyhood and grew precariously into a delicate, undersized little boy. We can imagine how his mother and elder sisters must have cosseted him, how anxiously his father must have watched over him. But however much he was indulged, he could not have been spoiled in the true sense of the word, for he grew up sweet-tempered and considerate of those around him. Right from the start, it was obvious that he was outstandingly intelligent, and he had the precious gift of keeping himself occupied and amused.

When Christopher was two and had a baby sister, life changed dramatically for the Wrens.

Dr. Wren was a very able man, too able, it was thought, to remain for long the rector of a quiet country parish. He was a Doctor of Divinity and had previously been domestic chaplain to the Bishop of Winchester. Even more significant, he was younger brother to Matthew Wren, Dean of Windsor. Windsor Castle is one of the chief residences of the kings and queens of England, and to be Dean of Windsor is to be in close touch with royalty. Matthew Wren was an awe-inspiring and important figure in the lives of the Wren children. They heard from their father how Uncle Matthew had been chosen especially by His Majesty King James I to be personal chaplain to his son Charles and to accompany him to Madrid to sue for the hand in marriage of the Infanta of Spain. This was a hazardous undertaking, as there was little love lost between Spain and England, and many people were puzzled at the King's motives in seeking such an alliance. However, the attempt was made. It was a failure, but that was no fault of Uncle Matthew's. He guarded and guided the young prince as he had been instructed to do, and the story of this adventure became a legend, we may be sure, to the young Wrens.

And now, in the year 1634, Uncle Matthew had his reward. He was given the Bishopric of Ely, in Norfolk, a county of wide, flat acres surrounding the soaring towers of one of the most beautiful cathedrals in England, and he was able to arrange for his younger brother, Christopher, to step into his shoes and become Dean of Windsor in his place.

Here was exciting news for the Wrens! Christopher must have been puzzled by the upheaval in the large old rectory as trunks were hauled down from the attics, packed, and loaded onto wagons to make their way along the rough, muddy roads over the Wiltshire Downs to Windsor, where the great walls and towers of the castle look down on the river Thames, and the city of London throbs with life not many miles away. Then one day the big family coach drew up at the door and little Kit, as he was called, left the old rectory and the garden he had just begun to explore. Who traveled in the coach, we wonder. We may imagine it packed to capacity with children, nursemaids, Mrs. Wren herself, perhaps the family pets. Dr. Wren probably chose to ride. A lumbering, unsprung coach containing a young infant, a restless toddler, and several little girls would hardly be the choice of a middle-aged, bookish man. Probably he went on ahead to see that everything was ready for them when they arrived.

Christopher was still too young to appreciate the way the family had risen in the world, but Susan, the eldest girl, would have been very conscious of the change. From a humble country parson, Dr. Wren had become a member of the court. They would have to be prepared to receive important guests at the deanery; he himself would be called upon to preach before the King.

The deanery was a substantial house, and it had need to be, for more babies arrived to fill the nursery and keep little Kit company. They were all girls, however, so Christopher retained his position as the only son of the house. In all, Dr. and Mrs. Wren had eleven children, although not all of them lived past infancy.

What sort of a home was it in which young Christopher and his sisters grew up? We know from letters and diaries of the time that the standard of living in the early seventeenth century was already much higher than had been considered comfortable and acceptable in the century before. The sixteenth century had been a time of great domestic change. Houses that had been built primarily as fortresses, with thick walls, small windows, and moats, changed by degrees into places much nearer to our ideas of home. In the country the peasants still lived in hovels that today we would consider unsuitable even for livestock, but farmers lived more comfortably, in houses of brick and stone, many of which still stand. The large landowners—the aristocracy—lived, very often, like princes, in huge mansions surrounded by miles of park and woodland, waited on by an army of servants. They were lords of all they surveyed, admitting no authority over them except that of their king and their church. Soon, both were to suffer an eclipse; after the Civil War, nothing was ever to be quite the same again. But when the Wren family settled into the deanery, these events were still in the future, and no hint of trouble to come disturbed young Christopher's placid life.

The fortunes of the Wren family were riding high. Dr. Wren was appointed Registrar of the Most Noble Order of the Garter. He was given the living of Hasely, in Oxfordshire. He put in a curate to do the work of the parish for him, as he had already done at East Knoyle. It was quite usual for the rector to be an absentee. He drew the stipend and paid the curate, and the difference in the two amounts went to help maintain a grand establishment and a large family.

This, then, was the situation of the Wren family in those last days before civil war tore their world apart. Comfortable, cultured, well-to-do, they were the staunchest Royalists. Their religion was High Church, and their king was second only to God. With indignation rather than, at first, alarm, they heard the rumblings that were to end in the landslide of war. They heard with incredulous anger of an attack on St. Paul's Cathedral, of a mob of fanatics threatening the Archbishop at Lambeth Palace, of Archbishop Laud, whom they venerated only second to the King himself, being thrown into the Tower of London. Under their secure lives the ground was beginning to shake. But for the present, life in the deanery went on as usual.

Until he was nine years old, Christopher was taught at home by a tutor, the Reverend William Shepheard. It was unusual to keep a boy at home for so long, but Kit's health was the excuse, and perhaps Dr. Wren was glad of a reason for keeping his only son at his side a little longer. Kit must have been an interesting companion even at that early age. He and his father shared the same curiosity to find out how things were done; the same practicality, which made them both wish to turn their ideas into tangible shape. Dr. Wren had already tried his hand at architecture in the church at East Knoyle, where he had made several improvements. Christopher was not the first of his line to fall under the spell of beautiful buildings.

But building was still far in the future for Kit Wren. His great interest, starting when he was a boy and lasting for a large part of his life, was astronomy. At that time, sundials were a useful part of everyday life. Clocks and watches had been in use for a long time, but they were not available to every man, whereas a sundial set up in a garden or on the wall of a building was useful to all—provided the sun shone. A watch sent man's gaze traveling downward and limited his vision; the sundial encouraged him to look upward and study the sky. Was the sun about to shine out of the clouds so that they might read on the dial how the day was passing? And once the habit of looking up was formed, how rewarding was the study of the heavens, what richness of mystery was there! "Dialing," as it was called, became the hobby of many thinking men, and it must have been in the garden of the deanery at Windsor that young Kit, held up perhaps by big sister Susan, first watched the shadow fall on the dial.

In 1642, the year in which Kit left the tranquillity of

home and plunged into the busy world of Westminster School, a shadow fell on England, the shadow of that most terrible of all conflicts, civil war.

Christopher had lived through nearly ten happy, secure years. He had been surrounded by a loving family, supported by his father's high position, stimulated by the many visitors who came to their house. The deanery had seemed invulnerable. The Dean, his brother the Bishop of Ely, and all other staunch High Churchmen, lived under the protection of the King. That the King had been ruling with a high hand, insisting upon his "divine right" in order to have his own way in all things, had long been a cause for concern. But to a small boy more interested in the stars and the wonderful models he had begun to make out of pasteboard, the outbreak of war must have come as a shattering blow. And this blow was closely followed by two more. Dr. Wren was expelled from the deanery and Uncle Matthew Wren was imprisoned in the Tower. Christopher's peaceful childhood ended abruptly. Homeless, the Wren family was to live for the next six and a half years in the shadow of fear.

To understand what led the country into the horror of civil war, it is necessary to look at the way society was changing in the new century. To begin with, the people were weary of the constant wars with foreign powers. Wars cost money, and as weapons became more sophisticated, the cost of war rose. In theory, the King owned the country, and if he needed money, then it was the duty of his subjects to provide it for him. James I made it abundantly clear that what he wanted, he would have, and no argument.

"As it is atheism and blasphemy to dispute what God can do," he said, "so it is presumption and high contempt in a subject to dispute what a king can do." Fine words, but the sentiment behind them was eventually to bring his son, Charles I, to the block.

Money talks, they say, and in this case it talked through the mouths of rich men, the aristocracy, living like princes on their huge estates. They set a limit on what they were prepared to pay out to the King and his ministers. They were more interested in conditions at home than in foreign affairs. The King might squabble with his neighbors over the water, but for themselves they preferred to spend their money on improving their estates, on rich clothing, jewels, horses, hounds, and good living.

The revolution which took place between 1640 and 1660 may have stemmed, as some believe, from religious conviction, or it may have resulted from economic pressure. Both probably contributed to the unrest. When a proud and stubborn king falls foul of his proud and stubborn subjects, something has to give, and in this case what eventually gave was the monarchy. The people had behind them the strength of Magna Carta, the Great Charter, which rejected the power of the king to control the personal property and liberty of citizens, except with the consent of that man's equals. Magna Carta had been dearly won; no Englishman then or now would consent to have it set aside.

With the death of James I in 1625, there could have been an easing of the situation. But his son, Charles, came to the throne determined to rule, as his father had done, with a high hand. For eleven years he refused to call a parliament, and the dissatisfaction and unrest, denied the outlet of free speech, grew and festered. And the times produced the man, as they always do—Oliver Cromwell, the Puritan who hated the monarchy and all it stood for. A towering figure by any standards, Oliver Cromwell was destined to rise to great heights of power and to leave marks on the country which survive to our own time.

This, then, was the state of England when Christopher went as a boarder to Westminster School in London. Dr. Busby was the headmaster. Himself a Royalist and a High Churchman, he took care to see that the tone of the school followed his convictions. This was no new thing for Christopher, who came from a home with similar beliefs. Dr. Busby was a formidable man, but he was a good schoolmaster and Christopher got on well with him, keeping up an affectionate friendship with him in later life. He spent three years at Westminster, working hard, while around him the country dissolved in tumult. If anything is needed to prove the incredible tenacity and single-mindedness of this boy, we have it here, in the progress he made in his studies while his private world was turned upside down and much that he held dear disappeared forever.

2

The Inventive Schoolboy

When Dr. Wren was turned out of the deanery in 1642, he fled with his family to Bristol, which was held for the King. They stayed there for three years, the years that Christopher was away at school. Christopher managed to get home occasionally for holidays, but it was a hazardous journey, and it must have been a constant anxiety for his father to have him so far from home. While they were at Bristol, news came to Dr. Wren of the ransacking of the deanery by Cromwell's troops. They took the Dean's own books and valuables, which he had had to leave behind in their sudden and urgent flight. What worried him even more was the news that they had looted the chapel and removed documents and registers belonging to the Order of the Garter, for which the doctor, as registrar, was responsible. Much later he was to regain possession of some of these books, which he hid until he died, passing on the secret of their hiding place to Christopher. Later, at the restoration of the monarchy, Christopher returned them to the Order. The new Dean of Windsor gave a receipt, which Christopher treasured and kept among his papers, to be passed on, in turn, to his own son.

> I do acknowledge that I have received from Mr Chris: Wren the son of Mr Dean Wren, a Box, in which are three Register Books, and other Note-books, all relating to the most noble Order of the Garter; in Testimony whereof, I have hereto set my Hand, this 11th day of August, in the year 1660.
>
> (*Signed*) BRUNE RYNES.

But all this was far in the future. Now, while Christopher studied at Westminster, mastering the classics and becoming deeply immersed in the study of astronomy and other sciences, one good thing at least happened to the Wren family. Susan married William Holder, a young clergyman who was at that time a don at Pembroke College, Cambridge. Pembroke was Dr. Wren's old college, which was a tie between him and his son-in-law; but all the family liked William for his own sake. He was a clever, attractive man, very fond of music and intensely interested in mathematics. He was to play a big part in Christopher's development, for, during holidays from Westminster, they worked together on this subject, which was not at that time taught in public schools. Christopher must have welcomed the entry of a young man into the family, a family so overweighted by the female side, and he and William became close friends.

Besides mathematics, William Holder explored what he called the "science of speech." He taught a deaf-and-dumb boy to speak and wrote papers on the subject, to be read before learned societies. Later in life, when he, like Dr. Wren, became a dean of the church, he was so strict a disciplinarian that his subordinates nicknamed him Mr. Snub Dean.

He did not, however, snub his clever young brother-in-law. Christopher had an unchildlike turn of mind that made him stimulating company even for a brilliant man.

It was well for Dr. Wren that he had a dependable son-in-law to support him in his troubles, for in 1643 another blow fell. Mrs. Wren died, shortly after the birth of her eleventh child. William and Susan went to live with the bereaved family at Bristol and finally made a home for them at Bletchington, not far from Oxford, where William had just been appointed rector. This move, however, could not be made until later, for Oxfordshire was overrun by Cromwell's troops and it was safer for Royalist sympathizers to stay with the garrison at Bristol until times changed.

While the family was at Bristol, the news came through that the deanery at Windsor had been looted a second time and that the Dean had been deprived of his living at Hasely. This was a serious blow to his purse as well as to his pride.

There remained East Knoyle, and there, when Bristol surrendered to Cromwell's troops in the autumn of 1645, the Wren family retreated. It must have been a dreary return to a spot where once they had been so happy, and they did not stay long. Soon, Bletchington rectory became available and they were able to settle down in relative peace and quiet. In the same year, 1646, Christopher, then thirteen, left Westminster School, and the family was reunited under William Holder's roof.

The move to Bletchington opens a new chapter in the lives of Dr. Wren and his son. To the doctor it brought peace after years of strain. It was rather a melancholy peace, for his brother was in the Tower; the King, to whom he gave his allegiance, was three years later put to death; and Oliver Cromwell, whom he saw as evil personified, went from strength to strength. The old man did not live to see the restoration of the monarchy, and when he died, it seemed as if the Lord Protector, as Cromwell was called, was unassailably secure. Dr. Wren had lived for nearly seventy years and must often have felt that his life had been a failure, but he left behind him a son so gifted that through his fame the father's name lives on.

To Christopher, Bletchington stood for stability and happiness. Susan was a second mother to him, and William was never too busy to help his young brother-in-law with his studies and schemes. The diarist John Aubrey has something to say about William Holder that helps us to picture him more clearly. He was, says Aubrey, "a handsome, graceful person of delicate constitution, very helpful in the education of his young brother-in-law, a youth of prodigious inventive wit of whom he was as tender as if he had been his owne child." Aubrey mentions that it was Holder who gave Christopher his "first instruction in Geometrie and Arithmetique" and, when he was a young scholar at the University of Oxford, was a very necessary and kind friend.

Aubrey has something to say about Susan too. He was writing much later, when Kit was Sir Christopher and had already risen to the public notice and was *persona grata* at court. Wrote Aubrey:

> It ought not to be forgot the great and exemplary love between this Doctor [Holder] and his virtuose wife, who is not less to be admired in her sex and station than her brother, Sir Christopher, and, (which is rare among women) her excellences do not inflate her. Among many other gifts she has a strange sagacity as to curing of wounds, which she does not doe so much by precedent and receipt books as by her own excogitancy, considering the causes, effects, and circumstances.

Susan, no doubt, had her herb garden at Bletchington and studied intelligently the use of herbal remedies, as did most women of her time and class. She put her knowledge to good use on one occasion when, Aubrey tells us in his gossipy way, "King Charles II had hurt his hand and the surgeon could do nothing for his relief. Then someone told the King what a rare shee-surgeon he had in his house; she was presently sent for at 11 o'clock at night: she made ready a pultisse and applyed it and gave his Majestie sudden ease and he slept well." Soon she had cured him, "to the great grief of all the surgeons who envie and hate her," concludes Aubrey wryly.

It seems from this that the Holders were at that time in residence at one of the palaces. This inclusion of the Wrens and the Holders in the charmed circle of the court was of the greatest help to Christopher in furthering his career. Staunch loyalty to the monarchy in time of trouble eventually brought rich rewards.

Susan's skill at healing would have been very useful during the time Christopher was at the rectory. He was endlessly inventive and was never content merely to theorize. He liked to see his theories take shape, and he spent hours making models in wood and pasteboard. No doubt, sometimes the knife would slip and Susan would have to bandage a cut finger. Even at school, Christopher was busy with his modelmaking. When he was twelve, he sent his father an "astronomical instrument," together with some verses in Latin. If this sounds advanced for a boy of twelve, it must be remembered that, from an early age, every gentleman's son was expected to be able to write Latin verse.

We can imagine with what pleasure Dr. Wren received these thoughtful gifts. Another, private grief had to be borne at about this time. One of the girls, Elizabeth, died of consumption at the age of eleven. She was just one year younger than Christopher and may very well have been his favorite in their nursery days, since they were almost of an age. There were so many things that could cause a child's death at that time, and so little protection from them. How anxiously Dr. Wren must have awaited Christopher's letters from school, for the boy was still far from strong. The sad, aging man and the clever boy were perfectly in sympathy with each other. They both loved and venerated beautiful things and both suffered when news came of the wanton damage done by Cromwell's soldiers. Cromwell, in common with many men of his beliefs, mistrusted beauty, believing it to be a snare of the devil's to distract men's minds from God. He turned a blind eye to the havoc wrought by his troops, who pulled down statues and burned paintings that belonged to the churches, on the grounds that they were Popish; destroyed rich men's houses for the pleasure of destroying; and chopped up valuable furniture for firewood. Even St. Paul's Cathedral suffered at their hands: troopers' horses were stabled in the nave.

No wonder that Christopher, growing up in the midst of turmoil, turned for relief to a study of the exact sciences. Up in the night sky was order and beauty untouchable by man. Later he became absorbed in medical experiments, but his first and greatest love was astronomy, and if he had died before he ever designed a building at all, he would still be remembered for the work he did in this field. We think of him as a great architect, as indeed he was, but for many years he thought of himself as an astronomer, and he never lost his interest in the subject throughout his long, full life.

It was while Christopher was still at school that his father, in London for a visit, introduced him to Sir Charles Scarborough, who, although only thirty, was already well known in the medical profession. He had been a Fellow of Caius College, Cambridge, but had been expelled on account of his loyalty to the King. Although mathematics were not part of the curriculum at the universities, Scarborough, together with his friend Seth Ward, had spent a good deal of time studying the subject. Having come across a most helpful book entitled *Clavis Mathematicae,* they sought out the author, William Oughtred, who gladly helped them with the difficult task they had set themselves. Oughtred was a great scholar who delighted in the company of the two intelligent young men, and a lasting friendship sprang up among the three. Oughtred put it on record that Charles Scarborough's memory was so good that he could "recite all the propositions of Euclid and Archimedes and apply them." Young Christopher was fortunate to be drawn into this magic circle of scholarship, and he seems to have spent a good deal of time in Sir Charles's own home as a kind of laboratory assistant, preparing and dissecting anatomical specimens.

About this time Christopher was ill. We have no account of what the trouble might have been, but Sir Charles Scarborough took charge of him and pulled him through. When he was well again, Christopher wrote to his father (in Latin, as usual) telling him all the news.

> *Honoured Father,*
>
> I am greatly enjoying the society of the famous Physician, [Sir Charles Scarborough] who is most kind to me; so gracious and unassuming is he as not to disdain to submit those Mathematical Studies in which he has so distinguished himself to what I will not call my Judgement but rather my Taste, so that he even lends a patient Ear to my Opinions and often defers to my poor Reasonings; while, in my turn, I impart to him anything of merit which I have lit upon or which I owe to you in Organics or Mechanics: one of these Inventions of mine, a Weather clock namely,

with Revolving Cylinder, by means of which a Record can be kept through the night, he asked me but yesterday to have constructed in brass at his Expense.

The other day I wrote a treatise on Trigonometry which sums up as I think, by a new method and in a few brief rules, the whole Theory of Spherical Trigonometry. An Epitome of this I re-wrote on a brass disc of about the size of one of King James's Gold Pieces, and having snatched the tool from the engraver, I engraved much of it with my own hand which Disc Sir Charles had no sooner seen than he insisted upon having a similar one of his own.

You know that there exists in the vulgar tongue a most esteemed Tract by Dr Oughtred on Geometrical Dialling which Tract the Author (worn out with years) has often besought Sir Charles to render into Latin, but he, with weightier Business in Hand, appointed me to the task which I have just completed. I shall now only add a Letter to the Author so that, to my great advantage, as Sir Charles promises, I may both gain an old Man's Favour, and, at the same time win that of all those Students of Mathematics who acknowledge Dr Oughtred as their Father and Teacher.

This letter leaves us gasping. Christopher, at the time, was barely fifteen, and his knowledge of mathematics had been gained by what must have been only sporadic teaching from his brother-in-law. Just consider the achievements he lists here, modestly but with barely concealed and very natural pride.

He invents a "weather cock," which Sir Charles insisted upon having constructed in brass. He writes a treatise on trigonometry, a shortened version of which he engraves with his own hands on a brass disk. He translates a learned tract into Latin, which was the common language among the educated; thus, learned men of every country could talk and write to one another without difficulty. Presumably, then, this would make the tract available to foreign students of mathematics who could not read English.

Sir Charles obviously found Kit Wren a valuable assistant in spite of his youth, and he certainly had Christopher's interests at heart, since he made it possible for him to win an "old Man's Favour."

Once the translation of the tract was finished and the letter written to tell his father all about it, Christopher gave his mind to composing a letter to the great Dr. Oughtred, and he put his heart and soul into the composition. He begins:

> To the Venerable Author of the Key well-termed Golden, to him of whose achievements in higher Geometry his Time must ever be proud, greeting. Welcome indeed, (most gifted of men) was the Shining of your Key upon the Sphere of Mathematics in this Age of ours . . .

To us this style sounds flowery and even insincere, but it was the custom of the times to be flowery and, compared with some contemporary letters, Christopher is being positively restrained.

The tract, he goes on to say, is regarded by the learned as a guiding light, since "led by thee they have been able safely and surely to cross the great stormy ocean of algebra and so attained to other and unexplored Regions of Mathematics." This reference to the great, stormy ocean of algebra will undoubtedly strike a chord of sympathy in the hearts of many readers. The dividing years roll away and we feel very close to the schoolboy who struggled with "math" more than three hundred years ago.

After comparing the tract to a star, for the stars were never very far from his mind, Christopher goes on to pay graceful tribute to his patron, Sir Charles.

> It is to his Kindness and Liberality of Mind that I am indebted not alone for any little skill I can boast in Mathematics, but for Life itself which, when suffering from recent sickness, I received from him as from the Hand of God.

Toward the end, the letter contains a rather amusing hint of criticism, which must surely have made the great man smile.

> I have therefore endeavoured to render your Treatise of Clocks almost Word for Word (this was the easier perhaps since you wrote it for practical use and therefore a little carelessly.)

The letter finishes, however, in the prevailing fashion of exaggerated humility.

> I was only fearful lest, owing to Ignorance of mine, one Point of Learning should be lost, Learning to be the humblest seeker after which I consider my proudest boast only asking of you (if even this be not more than I deserve) that you include among your most devoted admirers,
>
> CHRISTOPHER WREN

3

Gentleman Commoner

WHEN CHRISTOPHER was in his seventeenth year, two things happened that made a deep impression on him and on his life. In February 1649, King Charles I, defeated by Cromwell, lost his head on the block at the hands of his own people. The effect of this ghastly event on a boy whose father had always been a loyal monarchist and had brought him up to be the same can easily be imagined. To take the life of the King was to him, as to all other Royalists, treason of the worst sort, hardly better than blasphemy, since the King was also head of the church. Christopher was shocked and horrified, and it was well that he soon had something new to occupy his mind. In April he went up to Wadham College, Oxford, as a Gentleman Commoner.

For three years he had been visiting Oxford at intervals and may even have studied there from time to time, as some authorities claim that he joined the college in 1646, when he was barely fourteen. However, the records of Wadham College show that he entered in 1649, and this seems a more likely date, both because of his age and because he had spent so much time with Sir Charles Scarborough after leaving school. It seems reasonable to suppose that he left Westminster early (he was only thirteen) because he had learned all the masters could teach him and there was no point in staying longer. Remember, only the classics were taught, and Christopher, precocious as he was, was fluent at thirteen in Latin and Greek. Being too young for the university, he divided his time between William Holder's rectory, where he studied mathematics with his brother-in-law; Sir Charles's establishment in London, where he made himself generally useful, met influential people, and gathered information on a variety of subjects; and Oxford, where the Wrens had many friends, including Dr. John Wilkins, the Warden of Wadham College.

Dr. Wilkins had been private chaplain to a German prince, Charles Lewis, a nephew of Charles I and a frequent visitor, with his brother Prince Rupert, to the English court. Both the princes had visited at Dr. Wren's deanery, Rupert staying there as a house guest on several occasions. When Charles Lewis returned to Germany, Dr. Wilkins, who, in spite of his royal patronage, had Puritan leanings, was appointed to the post at Wadham by Cromwell. Cromwell, at the end of the Civil War, was turning out many of the men in high places who had Royalist sympathies and replacing them with men of his own choice. Besides Dr. Wilkins, he appointed Seth Ward to be Professor of Astronomy and John Wallis to be Professor of Geometry. Ward and Wallis both had a deep influence on Christopher and later worked closely with him.

That the university was in urgent need of a good "spring cleaning" there can be no doubt. During the war the town had first been the headquarters of the Royalist army. Cromwell's soldiers had besieged the Royalists, eventually forced them to surrender, and then occupied the town. Siege, surrender, occupation—nothing could be more catastrophic to the quiet atmosphere of a university town. Some of the inhabitants, notably the shopkeepers, tailors, and the like, had done very well indeed out of the wealthy followers of the King and the members of his court. But the number of scholars had dwindled, and of those that remained, many of them, in the words of a contemporary observer, were found to be "debauched by bearing armes and doing the duties belonging to soldiers, as watching, warding and sitting in tippling houses for whole nights together."

The Oxford at which Christopher arrived officially in 1649 was, then, in a state of transition. The same could be said of Christopher himself, who had spent the last three years in what someone who knew him described as a "strange interlude." Neither schoolboy nor adult, he had been accepted on almost equal terms into most exalted company, the company of brilliant men. It must have been a heady experience for what we would today call a teen-ager, but Christopher seems to have taken it all in his stride. His modesty and charm made him pleasant company, and his exceptional talents earned him the respect of everyone with whom he came in contact. During his time with Sir Charles Scarborough, he made pasteboard models demonstrating the working of the muscles in the human body—models that were used by Scarborough in his lectures at Surgeon's Hall. He helped with dissections too, and for a time physiology almost took the place of astronomy as the absorbing interest of his life. He took time off from medical affairs, however, to invent an instrument for writing with two pens at once, a very useful device for copying documents in the days before typewriters and carbon paper. Later, when he came to take out a patent for his "diplographic pen," he found he had a rival who claimed to have been first with the invention. Christopher was indifferent. He called the device "obvious though useful" and had to be persuaded to stand up for his rights. This attitude was typical of him all his life. Once a problem was solved, an invention—and he was endlessly inventive—perfected, he lost interest. It was finished; now he would start something new. Because of this, he did not always get full credit for what he did, and this upset his friends, who were more ambitious for him than he was for himself.

What sort of life would Christopher have led at Oxford? The curriculum was still almost medieval, and all work, of course, was done in Latin. This would not have bothered Christopher. He would have had a tutor and have attended lectures in grammar, rhetoric, dialectic, and moral philosophy. He would write essays on the subject matter of the lectures and submit these to his tutor, just as Oxford undergraduates do today, although now the subjects cover a much wider field. He would have had to "respond and oppose" at formal "Disputations," or debates.

His chief study at Oxford was astronomy. He spent a good deal of his time not only writing about the subject, but making practical working models of the heavens, demonstrating the solar system. We can imagine Christopher's rooms at Oxford being the despair of whoever had the task of keeping them clean. They would have been littered with pasteboard, colored inks, glue pots, and all the paraphernalia of the modelmaker, none of which he would permit to be dusted or disturbed.

His position as a Gentleman Commoner gave him certain advantages over the ordinary undergraduates. Gentleman Commoners dined at the Fellows table, where the conversation was probably very much to Christopher's sober taste, though this privilege understandably set up a barrier between the Commoners and the rest of the young men. That would have bothered Christopher very little, however, because he was immediately accepted, young as he was, into a charmed circle of older men, all with scientific interests like his own. Dr. Wilkins was a member of what had come to be known as the "Invisible College," that forerunner of the Royal Society of which Christopher was later to be a vital part.

The Invisible College met weekly in London to exchange notes on the experiments the members had made. It was, and is to this day, a sort of clearing house for scientific thought. While Dr. Wilkins was with Prince Charles Lewis in London, it was an easy matter for him to attend the meetings, which he greatly enjoyed. But when he was appointed to Wadham, it became impossible, and so he started meetings of his own in Oxford. Here, as in London, any discussion of religion or politics was barred absolutely. Only by doing this was it possible for men of both parties to meet and give their minds to the work which, to all of them, was too important to be hindered by quarreling. It was to prove of immense value to the country that they were able to do this, and do it they did. Christopher himself made close friends of many men who were neither churchmen nor Royalists but who shared his profound interest in astronomy, mathematics, and medical science. This "Experimental Philosophical Clubbe," as they called it, was probably the most important thing that happened in Oxford that century and certainly the most important influence in young Christopher's life.

Dr. Wilkins occupied what is known in the university as a "set" of rooms, all along the front of his college, on the first floor, and he gave one of these rooms, situated over the main gate and with a pleasant oriel window, to Seth Ward, the Professor of Astronomy, where he was joined by his ardent young pupil, Christopher Wren. This was known then and long afterward as the "astronomy chamber," and in this room much important work was done. John Wallis, Professor of Geometry, although not a Wadham man himself, spent a good deal of time there, establishing a firm friendship with young Christopher, and it was through Wallis that Christopher first turned to architectural problems.

It came about like this: Wallis, the new Professor of Geometry, invented a "geometrical flat floor." He had a model constructed to demonstrate how he had—by mathematics—solved the problem of supporting a floor, the area of which is wider than the lengths of the timbers available for joists (the supports on which the actual planks of the floor are laid). This practical application of mathematics to a building problem aroused widespread interest. Wallis lectured on it, with the aid of his model, on more than one occasion, and we can be sure Christopher attended these lectures. Later, when he came to design his first large building, the Sheldonian Theatre in Oxford, he adapted Wallis's floor and used it on a large scale.

Christopher enjoyed his time as a Gentleman Commoner enormously, and this is hardly surprising, for the life he led was exactly suited to his tastes. How he got along with the other young men of his age, it is hard to say. There is no record of him indulging in the usual high-spirited behavior of undergraduates. His friends were the dons, the lecturers, and his mind was entirely occupied with studying, inventing, discovering. There was no time or energy left for drinking parties, picnics, horse racing, and the periodic sorties of "gown" against "town." It is difficult to imagine Christopher becoming embroiled in a street fight. The other young men must have looked upon him as something of a curiosity—but the English have always had a taste for curiosities. They take pride in one of their number who is "different," and love a true eccentric.

Christopher was never eccentric, but he was certainly different. Many other young men "up" at Oxford with him had excellent brains, and some of them left their mark on the world. Christopher's difference was his unique ability to translate theories into practical form, and this is the key to his whole remarkable life. It is this that was to bring him to the peak of his career, the rebuilding of St. Paul's Cathedral.

A hard-working, brilliant, sober young man—that was Christopher Wren during his Oxford years.

Up at Oxford with Christopher were two of his cousins, Thomas and Matthew, the sons of Uncle Matthew, Bishop of Ely, now imprisoned in the Tower of London. Thomas was studying medicine and had a great love of music, while Matthew was deeply embroiled in politics. He was, of course, a Royalist, and to be an active Royalist in those days of Cromwell's glory was to be in constant danger. Christopher worried about him. John Aubrey tells us of a nightmare Christopher had when he was spending a holiday at East Knoyle, presumably during the year his father spent at the rectory.

He "dreamed he saw a fight in a great market place which he knew not, where some were flying and others pursuing and among those who fled he saw a kinsman of his, who went into Scotland with the King's army. They heard in the country that the King was come into England, but whereabouts he was they could not tell. The next night came his kinsman to Knoyle Hill, and brought with him the disastrous news of Charles the Second's defeat at Worcester, 1651."

Christopher, like the rest of us, obviously could not resist telling people his more interesting dreams. This particular one shows clearly that, although the young Wren seems to have been absorbed in his studies and a bewildering number of activities, underneath he was in constant anxiety and grief at the state of the country, his father's misfortunes, and the death of the King. His youth—despite all his advantages, a host of interesting friends, and the fascination of his work—was overshadowed by sadness. One wonders if he would have worked quite so hard or become so absorbed in astronomical studies if he had not found in study a way of escape from unhappiness. He did not even have the comfort of religion; the Church was eclipsed as effectively as the beheaded King. The Puritans had their own stern form of religion and they put down all other forms with a merciless hand. The pomp and beauty of the High Church services were forbidden, and much else with them. "No Church permitted to be open," writes the diarist John Evelyn on Christmas Day, 1652, and on the following Ash Wednesday, which every good churchman kept as a day of mourning, he writes: "In contradiction to all custom and decency the Usurper Cromwell feasted at the Lord Mayor's, riding in triumph through the city."

These were wretched, frustrating times for the High Church Royalists, and they could only hold on grimly, praying for the day, still some years in the future, when the monarchy would be restored and men would be free to worship as they wished.

In 1651 Christopher graduated and could thence write the letters B.A., Bachelor of Arts, after his name. After another two years' study, he became an M.A., a Master of Arts, and was entitled to call himself Dr. Christopher Wren. It was a foregone conclusion that such a brilliant young man would be offered a fellowship, and to nobody's surprise, he was appointed a Fellow of All Souls, Oxford.

4

"The Clubbe"

WITH THE ENDING of student days, life became even busier for Christopher Wren. He spent much of his time preparing work to be presented to the Experimental Philosophical Society, and through the society he met many people who were to become lifelong friends and colleagues.

Robert Hooke was one of these. Younger than Christopher, he came to Christ Church, Oxford, in 1653 and joined the "Clubbe" two years later. Hooke was a slightly deformed young man from the Isle of Wight, which lies just off the south coast of England. He had much in common with Christopher, having been, like him, an inventive, endlessly curious child. He was sent to Westminster School, again like Christopher, although probably a little later; and having a marked talent for drawing and painting, he was apprenticed for a time, on leaving school, to Sir Peter Lely, the fashionable portrait painter of those days. It seems, however, that he liked the sciences more than the arts, for not long after arriving at Oxford he became laboratory assistant to Dr. Willis, helping him with his chemical studies. From there he went on to assist

Robert Boyle, a well-to-do Irishman who had a laboratory in the High Street, where he carried out valuable scientific work. Boyle was a prominent member of the "Clubbe," and it may well have been through him that Christopher and Hooke first met, though there was a family connection too. One of Christopher's sisters married into the Hooke family, and Robert later writes about Cousin Wren-Hooke.

These two clever young men struck up a close friendship, working together first in scientific matters and later in architecture.

It was while Christopher was at All Souls that his reputation began to spread from the university to the world outside. Sir John Evelyn, whose meticulously kept diaries give us such a wonderful picture of the seventeenth century, made a point of meeting this outstanding young man when he visited Oxford during a tour of the country in the summer of 1654.

They met in Christopher's room at All Souls after attending a musical entertainment in the college, an entertainment in which Christopher took no part, having little love of music. "After dinner," wrote Evelyn in his diary, "I visited that miracle of a youth, Mr. Christopher Wren."

Still another activity which fascinated both Christopher and John Wilkins at this time was the study of bees. Perhaps they kept their hives in the lovely college gardens, hives which must have attracted a great deal of attention, for they were quite different from the traditional, straw beehives then in general use.

Again, John Evelyn has left us a picture.

> He [Dr Wilkins] was the first who showed me the transparent apiaries which he had built like castles and palaces, and so ordered them one upon another as to take the honey without destroying the bees. These were adorned with a variety of dials and little statues, vases etc. and he was so abundantly civil on finding me pleased with them as to present me with one of his hives.

There is something very reassuring about this description of beehives. That the clever Dr. Wilkins and the "miracle youth" could unbend sufficiently to play about with "little statues and vases," let alone bee-sized sundials, is a warm, human touch. These additions to the hives were quite unnecessary but must havc been fun. The hives were obviously the forerunners of the kind used by beekeepers today, although it was many years before the old straw "skep" went out of fashion, together with the custom of stupefying the bees with smoke—and frequently killing them—before the honey could be taken.

Sir John Eveyln was not the only "notable" that Christopher met around this time. Quite by accident—and to a Royalist it must have been rather like meeting the devil himself—he was presented to the usurper Cromwell. It happened at the home of Cromwell's favorite daughter, Lady Claypole, in London. Dr. Wilkins had married Cromwell's widowed sister, Roberta French, and it was no doubt he who introduced Christopher to the Claypoles, the husband being very interested in mathematics. As we know, the members of the "Clubbe" did not allow differences of political opinion to keep them from exchanging views on scientific matters, and as Lady Claypole was a staunch churchwoman in spite of her father's stern religious creed, Christopher would have felt safe in dining at her home. Imagine his horror, then, when in the middle of the meal, who should walk in unannounced but Cromwell himself. He sat down sullenly without speaking a word of greeting—but his family was used to this sort of behavior and passed it off as well as they could.

Suddenly Cromwell, recognizing the brilliant young professor from Oxford, turned to Christopher and said abruptly: "Your uncle has been long in the Tower."

"He has so, sir," said Christopher, as politely as he could, adding, with perhaps an edge to his voice, "He bears his affliction with great patience and resignation."

"He may come out an' he will," grunted Cromwell.

Christopher was amazed and incredulous. "Will Your Highness permit me to take this from your mouth?" he asked.

"You may," said Cromwell, and if he smiled sardonically, Christopher was too excited to notice. He made his excuses to his hostess at the first possible moment and hurried to the Tower to tell his uncle that the long captivity was over.

Poor Christopher! Uncle Matthew, who had heard all this before, snubbed him severely for his simplicity in supposing that the affair could be resolved so easily. This was not the first time, thundered Uncle Matthew, that he had received the like information from that miscreant, but he "disdained the terms projected for his enlargement which were to be a mean acknowledgment of his [Cromwell's] favour and an abject submission to his detestable tyranny," adding that he was "determined to tarry the Lord's Leisure and owe his deliverance (which he trusted was not far off) to Him alone."

After this setdown, Christopher must have disliked the Lord Protector even more than before.

IN 1657 CHRISTOPHER took another step upward in his career. He was now twenty-four and enjoyed a growing reputation in the scientific world, so it was not surprising that, when Gresham College in London needed a Professor of Astronomy, Christopher was offered the post.

There was an observatory at Gresham College, as well as lecture rooms and laboratories, and the men on the staff were all eminent in their own fields and often in other fields as well. The Professors of Music and Rhetoric, Dr. Petty and Dr. Crowne, were both physicians, and Christopher himself might equally well have lectured in geometry. They were what one might call good, all-round men, which made them stimulating company. Mr. Laurence Rooke, who had been Professor of Astronomy, had taken over the Chair in Geometry, and Christopher was offered the vacant place. He hesitated before accepting.

He felt very young, and the knowledge that his predecessor would still be on the staff, no doubt watching him with an eagle eye, must have been daunting. Christopher made up his mind to refuse the post, but his friends thought he shouldn't. Those close to him knew that he was inclined to underrate his own abilities with a modesty that was part of his charm, but they also knew that once he had been persuaded to undertake something, he could be trusted to do it thoroughly. They were confident of his ability to make a success of this new work, and finally they induced him to accept.

Christopher gave a great deal of time and thought to his all-important inaugural address. This first appearance before the members of the college was a nerve-racking experience, for people judge so much on first impressions. What impression did he wish to give? He felt he must be modest because of his youth, and yet he must give an air of confidence in himself, to justify his appointment. It was the fashion to write and speak with great formality, but through the formal words there had to come sincerity of feeling.

"Looking with respectful Awe on this great and eminent Auditory," wrote Christopher carefully, "while there I spy some of the *politer genii* of our Age, there some of our Patricians, there many choicly learned in the Mathematical Sciences, and everywhere those who are more Judges than Auditors, I cannot but, with Juvenile Blushes, betray that which I must apologise for. And indeed I must seriously fear, but I should appear immaturely covetous of Reputation in daring to ascend the Chair of Astronomy . . . when it would better have suited the Bashfulness of my years, to have worn out more Lustre in a Pythagorean Silence."

There was a great deal more of this, and it was well received. The young man, everyone felt, had shown a very proper diffidence about his lack of years and experience, but that was all he did lack. His brilliance of mind made him a welcome colleague, and he soon settled down among friends, old and new, to do valuable work.

It was during his time at Gresham College that Christopher became particularly engrossed in medical science, so much so that, temporarily, it almost took precedence over astronomy. He, Dr. Willis, and Robert Boyle, the Irishman, carried out a series of experiments to prove that liquids introduced into the bloodstream could affect the brain. The theory of the circulation of the blood, as propounded by Harvey, was still fresh in men's minds, and Christopher and his colleagues were curious to know what would happen if the blood was made to carry different substances around the body and into the brain.

For their experiments they used dogs, and if this revolts us and makes us feel that they must have been unpleasant people to indulge in such cruel practices, it must be remembered that in those days operations were of necessity performed without benefit of anesthetics. Men had to submit themselves to the surgeon's knife while fully conscious, as Samuel Pepys did when he was "cut for the stone"; and what a man could bear, a dog, they believed, could bear more easily, since a dog has not the same highly developed nervous system as a man.

The dog used on this first occasion was a large cross-bred spaniel. A vein was opened in one back leg and opium mixed with wine was injected by means of a hollow quill. Within a very short time the dog stopped struggling against the straps that held him to the table and became semiconscious. He was untied and taken into the garden, where they ran him up and down to keep him awake. Presently he recovered, and showed no ill effects. (This experiment, and others of a similar nature with different substances, made the dog so well known that somebody thought it worth his while to steal him, and the famous dog was never seen again.)

Medical science was on the march, but old beliefs and superstitions died hard, even among enlightened men. John Aubrey tells a story about Christopher which shows an unexpected credulity.

> Strawberries have a most delicious taste and are so innocent that a woman in childbed or one in a feaver may safely eat them: but I have heard Sir Christopher Wren affirm that if one has a wound in the head eates them they are mortal. Methinks 'tis very strange.

One person who would have been delighted at Christopher's appointment to Gresham College was his father, but, sadly, he died just before the professorship was offered to his son. He was nearly seventy, and for the last sixteen years of his life he had known sorrow and deprivation. He had lost his deanery and both his country parishes; he had suffered the mental agony of seeing his country taken over by men he abominated and his King put to death. He had lost his wife and a much loved daughter. If it had not been for the unfailing kindness of his son-in-law, William Holder, and Susan's loving care, he would have been miserable indeed. But he was cherished in the rectory at Bletchington and he had Christopher's career to follow and Christopher's letters and visits to look forward to, so life was not entirely without meaning. At least he was better off than his brother Matthew, incarcerated for eighteen long years in the Tower.

Christopher had been hardly a year at Gresham College when Cromwell died. The Royalists' pleasure at the death of the man they hated was damped by the civil disturbances that followed his death. As so often happens after the death of a dictator, the country was thrown into confusion, a confusion that lasted for two years and made life very uncomfortable for learned professors who wished, first and foremost, to be left in peace to get on with their work.

There was no peace allowed to Christopher and his fellow professors at Gresham College. The premises were turned into barracks for soldiers and the professors dispersed. Christopher went back to Oxford. His friend Dr. Sprat wrote to him from London.

> This day, I went to visit Gresham College, but found the Place in such nasty Condition, so defiled, and the Smells

> so infernal, that if you should now come to make use of your Tube, it would be like Dives looking out of Hell into Heaven.

Christopher's "Tube" was probably some kind of periscope, for we know that one of his many inventions was "a way of submarine navigation."

Cousin Matthew Wren wrote at about the same time, and his letter confirmed Dr. Sprat's. He called at Gresham College, but ". . . at the gate I was stopped by a man with a Gun who told me there was no Admittance on that Account of the College being reformed into a Garrison."

It must have been a frustrating period for Christopher, a professor without a college. But, as usual, he had so many projects in mind, so many irons in the fire, that he had no time to sit and brood. The "Clubbe" went on meeting in Oxford; Christopher was shortly to publish a tract on the "Rectification of the Cycloid"; he was assisting Dr. Wallis with his medical experiments; he developed the barometer—some say he was the inventor, but it had, in fact, been invented ten years before by an Italian and completed by a Frenchman, Pascal.

About this time, too, Christopher and his friends had some rather highbrow fun with the French mathematicians who challenged the mathematicians of England to solve a problem that Pascal had set. A prize of twenty pistoles was promised to the successful competitor. Christopher solved the problem, but there is no record of his ever having received the prize.

Meanwhile, in the country at large, things were stirring and change was in the air.

In October of 1659 John Evelyn wrote in his diary:

> The Armie now turned out of Parliament. We had no Government in the Nation; all is confusion, no Magistrate either owned or pretended by the Souldiers, and they are not agreed. God Almighty have mercy on and settle us.

Evelyn was by now an intimate friend of Christopher's, and as he was very much in the know about public affairs, it is possible that he may have given Christopher some hints as to what was in the wind. He would surely have let him know that at long last Uncle Matthew was to be released. On March 15, 1660, Colonel Morley, Governor of the Tower, received curt orders from General Monk, who since Cromwell's death was in supreme command, to let the old man go.

It must have been with mixed feelings that Matthew Wren came back into the world. He was now seventy-five; most of his family and many of his friends were dead, and the church, for whose sake he had suffered his long imprisonment, was in a state of ruin. He had seen close friends taken out and executed; he had heard of the execution of his royal master; he had waited daily for death to come to him. His health was broken, but his faith still shone brightly—the only thing left to him, and the most important of all. During his long years in the Tower he had made a vow that if it should please God to restore him his patrimony, "he would return into Him by some holy and pious employment that summe and more which by way of His gracious providence was unexpectedly conveyed in unto me during my eighteen years captivity . . . from sundry noble and truly pious Christians."

As soon as he was released, he began working out a scheme for a chapel for Pembroke College, Cambridge, where he had studied in his youth. A few years later he was to ask his nephew, Christopher Wren, to draw up the designs and carry out his plan.

On May 8, 1660, Christopher, his heart full of happiness, heard the bells of Oxford peal their joyful message to a people sick and tired of Puritan rule. King Charles II had been proclaimed in London and the monarchy was restored.

Part II

BIRTH OF AN ARCHITECT

Thrice happy they, who first with souls refined,
To these pursuits their generous care confined,
Who, nobly spurning Earth's impure abodes,
Assayed to climb the mansions of the gods.
Foes to ambition, and her idle lure,
From thirst of fame, from thirst of gold secure.

OVID

5

The Royal Society

Charles II was not long in returning to his own country from Holland once he was proclaimed king. On May 29, his thirtieth birthday, he arrived in London, and the citizens went mad with joy. All the pent-up feelings of those repressive years were given expression in the welcome they prepared for their King. Writes Evelyn:

> . . . the wayes strewed with flowers, the bells ringing, the streetes hung with tapistry, fountaines running with wine, the Mayor, Aldermen and all the Companies in their liveries, chains of gold and banners; Lords and Nobles clad in cloth of silver, gold and velvet, the windows and balconies well set with ladies; trumpets, music, and myriads of people flocking, even so far as from Rochester, so as they were seven hours in passing the Citty, even from 2 in the afternoone till 9 at night. I stood in the Strand and beheld it and blessed God.

With the coming of the King, Gresham College was restored to its rightful use and Christopher returned there with the other professors, though only for a short time. Early in the following year he went to Oxford, the town which became, perhaps more than anywhere else, his home. In the fall of the same year, he was created Doctor of Laws, and Cambridge University conferred the same honor on him shortly afterwards.

Before Christopher left Gresham College, a very important though informal meeting took place in the astronomy professor's rooms, at which the idea was put forward of inviting the King to grant a charter to the society now formed by the London and Oxford branches of the "Experimental Physiological Clubbe." The King, as was well known, had a deep interest in scientific affairs. During his long exile he had often passed the time carrying out experiments. He could not have been a better man to approach, and as soon as he was approached, he readily agreed to give his patronage to what was in future to be known as the Royal Society.

This was a great day for the members of the "Clubbe." Dr. Sprat writes:

> Upon the Restoration of the King, Philosophy had its share in the Benefits of that glorious Action; for the Royal Society had its beginning in that Time when the Kingdom was freed from Confusion and Slavery, so in its Progress, its chief Aim hath been to redeem the Minds of Men from Obscurity, Uncertainty and Bondage.

Men of learning often felt that they did not receive the recognition due to them, being outshone by the men of action and their more spectacular achievements. In our own age, when radio, television, and the press constantly bring us news of scientific achievement, this is no longer the case. But in the seventeenth century learning was confined to a very small section of the public, and the men who strove to break through the barriers of ignorance had reason to feel that nobody knew, nobody cared. Because of this, the recognition of a scientific body by the King was of immense importance and spurred them on to further efforts.

With the return of the monarchy, England, released after twenty years from the stern, restraining hand of Puritanism, went a little mad. It is hardly surprising. The English are, on the whole, people who enjoy relaxation and take a deep pleasure in the arts. King Charles II, after long years of exile and deprivation, was determined to enjoy his new life as king, and his people, especially the Londoners, were only too ready to follow where he led.

During Cromwell's years of power, the palace of Whitehall, the King's London home, had been stripped of its riches. Charles set about restoring it to its former glory. He managed to reassemble many of the pictures that his father had collected and his enemies removed, and he had the pictures hung in what was called the Stone Gallery, which became a kind of National Picture Gallery, open to all comers. The public came in flocks, not only to see the pictures but to exchange news. The Stone Gallery became the hub of the city, a clearing house for rumors and gossip. Here, there was always a chance of seeing the King, even of gaining his attention for a moment as he passed through. With luck, he might pause to listen to a request or a grievance—although more often he hurried away, surrounded by his ministers, only calling a genial "God bless you! God bless you," to the thronging crowds as he went.

If one missed seeing the King in the Stone Gallery, there were other places where one was sure of a good view, provided one could push one's way in. Every day he dined in state, a little after midday, in the Banqueting Hall, and anyone could come and watch him eat, from the galleries above. Then on Sunday one could watch the King pray in the Chapel Royal and, after years of silence, enjoy organ music. The very first Sunday that the King was back in London, Uncle Matthew, Bishop Wren, newly released from the Tower, preached before him in all the glory of lawn sleeves and the rest of a bishop's vestments. There were crimson cushions for the King and the courtiers to kneel on, and cloth of gold on the communion table. To the people of London, starved for so many years of beauty and color, it was an intoxication even to hear about such things, let alone see them with their own eyes.

What must have pleased and encouraged Christopher and his circle more than the return of gracious living was the knowledge that the King had had constructed for his own use a laboratory in the palace of Whitehall. Here his own chemist, Le Febvre, carried out experiments, often concocting medicines with herbs from the Physic Garden inside the palace walls. Here the King loved to work, forgetting affairs of state as he probed, dissected, and analyzed. To have such a man as king was very much to the taste of the members of the Experimental Physiological Clubbe, now the Royal Society.

To the great majority of the English people the restoration of the monarchy and all that went with it was as if the sun had burst out from behind dark thunderclouds, but to those of the Puritan faith it was more as if the devil himself was loose in the land. There had been emigration to America steadily all through the century. Cromwell himself had considered emigrating to New England when he was a young man. One wonders what would have happened to England if he had. Now, with one whom they considered worldly and frivolous firmly on the throne, the Puritans left in flocks, bearing their stern self-discipline and rigid ideals to a land where they would be free to live as they wished and to worship soberly in the way they believed to be most pleasing to God.

England did not miss them. Life was full of bubbling excitement, so much was changing. And every day there was a new story about the King and his court.

> The King has brought many strange birds and animals into his park. He has planted flowers and walks of trees for everyone to enjoy.
>
> The King loves music. He allows the public to listen to his fiddlers. The King plays games, he loves hunting, he swims in the Thames.
>
> The King appreciates beautiful things. His palace is splendid in crimson and gold, with four thousand gilt mirrors from France and hangings of brocade.
>
> The King loves fine clothes, both for men and women. London is full of French fashions, full of wide-skirted coats with huge, embroidered cuffs, of gold and silver lace and elaborate, curled wigs.

> The King loves his little dogs, but they are perpetually stolen. It seems very hard if the King cannot keep his dogs, simply because they belong to him, and that gives them a special value to the thief.

Stirring, exciting times. But there is no evidence that Christopher, still in Oxford, allowed himself to be caught up in the craze for amusement which was such a natural reaction after the years of repression. While the King and his followers made merry with masques and balls, Christopher enjoyed himself more soberly. Released from the tension of national unrest, thankfully rid of a distasteful dictatorship, Christopher and his fellow scientists went from strength to strength. Never was there such an era of discovery and invention. At the back of this book is a list of just some of the "New Theories, Inventions, Experiments and Mechanical Improvements" which Christopher was working on at this time. The range of his knowledge is staggering. In this list, which Christopher called his "catalogue" and which was his first contribution to the new-found Royal Society, he seems to have gathered up all his past experiments and inventions, possibly improved them and set them in order. He has included the famous diplographic pen, and the weather clock, which was one of his first inventions when he was still a schoolboy. "New ways of graving and etching" probably had their beginnings when he snatched the metal disk out of the hands of the engraver and finished the work himself. The artificial eye and the Strainer of the Breath belong to his medical interests, and we get a hint of his future in "New Designs tending to Strength, Convenience and Beauty in Building."

Formidable as this catalogue is, however, it does not include one discovery of Christopher's which his friend Dr. Sprat considered most important—nothing less than the laws of motion. In his *History of the Royal Society,* he writes:

> In the whole Progress of this Narration I have been cautious to forbear commending the Labours of any private Fellows of the Society . . . but now I must break this law in the particular case of Dr Christopher Wren . . . for in turning over the Registers of the Society I perceived that many excellent things whose first invention ought to be ascribed to him were casually omitted . . . The first instance I shall mention, to which he may lay peculiar claim is the Doctrine of Motion . . . Dr Wren produced before the Society an Instrument to represent the Effects of all sorts of Impulses made between two hard, globous Bodies of different Bigness and Swiftness following or meeting each other or the one moving, the other at rest.

King Charles granted the charter in 1661 and the "Clubbe" became, officially, the Royal Society. The following year he presented the Society with a mace, "of silver, richly gilt," which at every meeting of the Society, right to the present day, is placed in front of the president before business can begin. And in the same year as the first charter, a second charter granted arms to the Society with the motto NULLIUS IN VERBA. This is taken from lines from Horace which in English go:

And do not ask, by chance, what leader I follow or what godhead guards me. I am not bound to revere the word of any particular master.

These words are very important if we are to understand the breaking away of the Royal Society from the traditional beliefs held by learned men up to that time. Formerly, the laws of ancient Greece had been the chief influence on all thought and learning, with Aristotle as the authority on scientific matters. The works of Galileo, Gilbert, and Kepler, men who departed from the thinking of the ancients, were not taught in the universities, but some men did admire those works, and it was these men who founded the Royal Society and who pledged themselves not to "revere the work of any particular master," but to keep an open mind. This was a tremendous step forward. It can be said that modern science starts there.

The first president of the Royal Society was Viscount Brouncker, a mathematician. Christopher was, of course, a founder member, together with his close friends Dr. Wilkins, John Wallis, Robert Hooke, Robert Boyle, Sir John Evelyn, and many others, forty in all. The subscription was one shilling a week, and the group met regularly, "to enlarge knowledge by observation and experiment."

Shortly before the granting of the royal charter, the King appointed a new Dean of Windsor, and Christopher had the bittersweet experience of returning to his old home to hand over to Dean Rynes the register and notebooks of the Garter which his father had saved and kept hidden for so long. It was saddening for him to see the damage done by Cromwell's troops to St. George's Chapel and the deanery, places that were full of memories of his parents and the happy days before the war. Still, the sorrow was overlaid with pleasure that work had already started on the chapel and that soon it would be restored to its former glory.

Christopher had little time to look back and sigh. The present was too full and the future too promising, for he had been offered a new post—one very much to his taste. His friend Seth Ward, Savillian Professor of Astronomy at Oxford, had been appointed Bishop of Salisbury, and the professorship thus left vacant was offered to Christopher. The following year, then, Christopher resigned his Gresham College post and took the Savillian Chair, although he still spent much of his time—some thought too much—in London.

His particular concern at that time was the moon. He set himself to the enormous task of making, to quote his own words, a "lunar globe, representing not only the spots and various degrees of whiteness upon the surface but the Hills, Eminences and Cavities moulded in solid work. The Globe thus fashioned into a true Model of the Moon as you turn it to the light, represents all the menstrual Phases with a Variety of Appearances that happen from the Shadow of the Mountains and Vallies."

This model attracted a great deal of attention in learned circles, as well it might, and news of it eventually reached the King. One day, to Christopher's mixed pleasure and consternation, he received a letter.

> *To Dr Wren, Savillian Professor of Astronomy at Oxford.*
>
> *Much Honoured Friend.*
>
> The King hath commanded us to lay a double charge upon you in his Name to perfect the Design wherein he is told you have already made some progress to make a Globe representing accurately the figure of the Moon as the best Tube represented; and to delineate by the Help of the Microscope the Figures of all the insects and small living creatures you can light upon . . .

This was an honor indeed, and Christopher was quite prepared to make a second globe—but to be asked to spend hours and hours in the tedious work of making microscopic drawings of "all insects and living creatures" was something else again! He had neither the time nor the inclination for this, and somehow he managed, tactfully, to wriggle out of it. A second letter, dated two months after the first, indicates that the easygoing King had relieved him of the task and assigned it to Robert Hooke.

King Charles was not a touchy man. He liked everyone around him to be happy and at ease, and he regretted that his subjects should feel so strongly about religion and other burning questions of the hour that they must be forever quarreling and dragging him into their quarrels. If the Professor of Astronomy did not want to make drawings for him, no doubt he had a very good reason. The King had suggested it only because Dr. Wren had given him a few drawings on a previous occasion and it had seemed a kindly gesture to ask for others. No matter. Let the young man bring his moon model to Whitehall. He was a very clever man, a valued subject of the Crown, and ought to be encouraged. He should present his model at a private audience, and it should have a place of honor in the royal cabinet.

So Christopher took his model to Whitehall and had a long talk with his royal patron about the activities of the Society. The model was placed in the royal cabinet, on a pedestal, which was inscribed:

TO CHARLES II
KING OF GREAT BRITAIN, FRANCE AND SCOTLAND,
FOR THE EXPANSION OF WHOSE DOMINIONS SINCE
NO ONE GLOBE CAN SUFFICE,
CHRISTOPHER WREN DEDICATES ANOTHER IN THIS
LUNAR SPHERE.

Nobody, not even Robert Hooke, toiling away at the microscopic drawings of insects in Christopher's place, grudged the Professor of Astronomy his triumph. Christopher had the happy knack of arousing admiration in his friends, rather than jealousy of his spectacular achievements.

> "One there is," said a fellow professor at Gresham in the course of a speech, "whose name common gratitude forbids me to pass over, whom I know not whether to admire for his divine genius or for the sweetness of his disposition . . . once a prodigy of a boy, now a miracle of a man, and, lest I seem to exaggerate, it will suffice if I name the great and good Christopher Wren . . ."

High praise indeed from a contemporary! It was very pleasant for the young Dr. Wren to know that he was held in such esteem by men many years his senior, but their high opinion carried with it certain penalties. Whenever there was something to be done that needed prompt action and sure judgment, they were apt to call on Christopher for help, even when the matter was not really in his line. It was left to him, for instance, to draw up the charter for the Royal Society to be submitted to the King, although he never laid any claims to being a writer. He did his best, however, and as usual his best was very good—according to the flowery fashion of the day. After the usual compliments to the King and references to the "Benignity of Heaven, which in the same Shower yields Thunder and Violets and no sooner shakes the Cedars but, dissolving the Clouds, drops Fatness," he slips in a very cunning reason for the royal patronage of the Society, commending to the King's notice "those Parts of it which concern the Increase of Commerce by the Addition of useful Inventions tending to the Ease, Profit or Health of our Subjects, which will be best accomplished by a Company of ingenious and learned Persons well qualified for this Sort of Knowledge to make it their principal Care and Study . . ." He is careful to add, however, in case it should be assumed that the Royal Society was to be only of commercial use: ". . . we purpose to make further Provision for this Branch of Knowledge likewise: natural experimental Philosophy."

And that, thought Christopher—and his fellow members agreed with him—should cover everything.

6

Dr. Wren, Professor of Astronomy

THE YEAR 1662 came in full of promise for young Dr. Christopher Wren. The King was now firmly in command of the country and conditions were returning to normal, from the Royalist point of view. Christopher had his professorship at Oxford to provide him with a living and the Royal Society to provide even such an insatiable seeker after knowledge as he with occupation and stimulating company. The Society met every week, and Christopher usually managed to be there, though the journey from Oxford to London was tedious and time-consuming. A little murmuring went on in Oxford about the Savillian Professor's frequent absences, but it never amounted to outspoken criticism. After all, the work the professor was doing under the auspices of the Royal Society reflected credit on the university, and there was no doubt that he was becoming very well known and was on easy terms with the King.

The King, however, was not having such an easy time as his fortunate subject, Christopher Wren. The King was beset by problems, the greatest of them being a lack of money. He was in deep financial difficulties. The navy needed thousands of pounds—some of the men had received no pay for years; the royal servants' wages were in arrears; a great deal of repairing and rebuilding had to be done. Things were so bad that Charles said ruefully that when people came to see him at Whitehall he could not even offer them a meal. The bakers were refusing to supply any more ship's biscuit to the fleet until they had been paid, and when the Queen Mother came over from Holland on a visit the captains reported that they did not have enough gunpowder for the royal salute. Things were very bad indeed. It was all very well for Parliament to promise to bring the King's income up to £1,200,000, but in actual fact, in that first year, £70,000 was all that he received.

There were other troubles, too. The King's young brother, Henry, Duke of Gloucester, died of smallpox, and his other brother, James, Duke of York, secretly married a commoner, Anne Hyde, a daughter of Lord Chancellor Hyde, who was furious when he heard of the match.

In the middle of all this, the Queen Mother arrived and had to be met at Dover and properly entertained. The only bright spot was that she brought with her Minette, Charles's youngest and favorite sister. He adored Minette and did everything he could to make her visit a pleasant one. The trouble was to find as much time to be with her as he wished, his days were so full of affairs of state. Once, in the middle of an important meeting, he pushed a piece of paper across the table to Chancellor Hyde.

> I would willingly make a visit to my sister . . . When do you think I can best spare time?

Hyde read this, added a line, and pushed the paper back.

> I suppose you will go with a light train?
>
> I intend to take nothing but my night bag [wrote the King].

Hyde looked concerned as he bent over the paper again. "You will not go without forty or fifty horse?"

The King smiled and scribbled a final line: "I count that part of my night bag."

No wonder his household expenses were high.

When a man finds himself very short of money, there is one way in which he may add to his income, and that is by marrying a rich wife. Charles began to look around for the right princess.

A fortnight after his coronation, which was a splendid affair and cost a great deal of money, Charles met his new Parliament and told them his choice of a bride. It had been a difficult decision to make. The Spanish were anxious that he should marry someone they approved of, promising to endow richly a suitable lady. They offered Saxon, Dutch, and German princesses, but Charles would have nothing to do with them. "Odd's fish, they are all foggy," he said impolitely, and made his own choice, a Portuguese princess with a magnificent dowry: Catherine of Braganza. He told Parliament:

> I have often been put in mind by my friends that it was high time to marry, and I have thought so myself ever since I came to England . . . I can now tell you, not only that I am resolved to marry, but whom I resolve to marry, if God please . . . and trust me, with a full consideration of my subjects as of myself, it is with the daughter of Portugal.

The King's marriage, which took place in the spring of 1662, was directly responsible for turning Christopher's thoughts toward architecture. Part of the rich dowry that the Princess brought to Charles was the town of Tangier on the North African coast, just across the straits that divide Africa from Spain. Charles discovered that the harbor and fortifications there were in a ruinous state and the defenseless town was wide open to invasion by the Moors. Something had to be done, and so, prompted by Sir John Evelyn, he asked Christopher to go out to Tangier to make a survey of the state of the town. He offered him a very handsome salary and a dispensation from his duties as Savillian Professor. Even better, he promised him the post of Surveyor-General of the King's Works, on the death of Sir John Denham, who held the post but was, the King assured Christopher rather callously, in failing health. This tempting offer was sent to Christopher in a letter from his cousin Matthew, now secretary to Lord Chancellor Hyde, and Matthew was disappointed and annoyed when Christopher, to everyone's surprise, turned the offer down.

Why he refused, we can only guess. The excuse he made was his health, and this may have had something to do with it. We know that as a child he was not robust. All the same, there is no record that he suffered from anything in particular once he had grown up, and certainly he lived to a ripe old age. One feels that there was more to it than this, and the clue lies, perhaps, in his temperament. Whatever work Christopher was engaged in at the time was all-important to him and he did not care to be disturbed. Not only that; he was often reluctant to take on anything new—although, once persuaded, he put his back into the job and made a success of it. Finally, he may quite simply have disliked traveling. He never did travel much in all his long life, and only once left England, to pay a prolonged visit to France. This seems to be the most likely explanation, and quite understandable, for traveling in the seventeenth century was fraught with discomfort and danger. It was not, however, a good reason to give the King, and so Christopher fell back on the time-honored excuse—poor health—but he "prayed his Majesty to command his services in England."

The King, luckily, did not take offense. He thought so highly of Christopher that in order to give him an official job in the royal service he created one for him—the post of assistant to the Surveyor-General, with the understanding that it would be only a question of time before he stepped into Sir John Denham's shoes. Denham, old and tired, was not sorry to have a young, able man as his assistant. There was a great deal of work to be done in his department, and he knew only too well that much of it was beyond his powers, for he had no special qualifications as an architect. St. Paul's Cathedral needed extensive repairs, Windsor Castle was in poor shape, and Greenwich Palace, which had been begun by the great architect Inigo Jones, was still to be completed.

It was rather odd that Christopher should have been chosen for this very exacting post. We, with hindsight, know that it was an inspired choice, and we must give Sir John Evelyn the credit for having realized this. But at the time it was a surprising appointment. Christopher, in the charter of the Royal Society, is described as "Doctor in Medicine, Saville Professor of Astronomy in our University of Oxford." Nothing he had done up to this time—if we exclude the beehives!—gave any indication that he would make a good architect. John Evelyn seems to have acted on a hunch, backed up by the knowledge that Christopher's father had taken an interest in building, making improvements both at East Knoyle and at Windsor, and taking into consideration Christopher's sound knowledge of mathematics, and his reputation for making a success of anything he was induced to undertake.

It was one of the most inspired hunches of all time.

CHRISTOPHER had no sooner taken up his new appointment than he was given two private commissions.

The first came from the new Archbishop of Canterbury, Gilbert Sheldon. During the past years the ceremony of conferring degrees, known as the "Act," had been carried out in the university church of St. Mary's, Oxford. Sheldon considered that using a church for a lay ceremony, however important, was desecration, and he decided to set matters right by building and presenting to the university a "theater" in which the Acts could be more properly held. He asked Christopher to design the building and allocated the sum, enormous in those days, of £16,000 for the purpose.

Christopher wasted no time. By the following year, 1663, he was exhibiting a model of the Sheldonian Theatre, as it was to be called, to the Royal Society.

The model excited a good deal of interest. In addition to using Dr. Wallis's geometrical flat floor on a gigantic scale (the interior of the building was 80 by 70 feet, one of the largest buildings of that time), Christopher had adopted the same principle to support the roof. Up to that time, a large roof span had been supported on pillars. In order to avoid pillars, which are a nuisance in a building where everyone wishes to have an uninterrupted view of the stage, Christopher devised timber trusses. Roof trusses are very well known today. Prefabricated in steel or reinforced concrete, they are used extensively in many types of building from barns up. But in the seventeenth century they were an entirely new idea and could have been conceived only by a mathematician with a knowledge of stresses and strains. It was this new concept that made the model of such interest to the Royal Society.

When Sir John Evelyn visited Oxford, he was shown

many new things, including the model of the theater. "That incomparable genius, my worthy friend Dr Christopher Wren," he writes in his diary, "showed me the model not disdaining my advise in some particulars." It was this sweetness of temper, this "not disdaining advise" from friends, which made Christopher so much loved.

The Sheldonian Theatre took time to build, and it was not completed until 1669. In the meantime, Christopher had other work on hand. His Uncle Matthew, Bishop of Ely, had not forgotten the vow he made on being released from the Tower. He was eager to build the memorial chapel at Pembroke College, Cambridge, and had, as it were, tried out his nephew's ability as an architect by having him design a doorway to the north transept of Ely Cathedral. Being satisfied with the work, he gave him the task of designing the chapel.

Christopher worked fast. He drew up plans to his uncle's satisfaction, and the foundation stone was laid in May 1663. The chapel was completed and consecrated two years later. But before that happened, Christopher was given something of greater importance to do in his official capacity as Assistant Surveyor-General.

He was summoned by the Dean and Chapter to survey St. Paul's Cathedral. On the day when he first walked around the melancholy and desecrated church, he began an association that ended only with his death.

NOW BEGINS A PERIOD in which Wren the architect gradually emerges from Wren the scientist and astronomer. He was still the Savillian Professor and remained so until 1673. He was still a tireless experimenter and inventor, and although his interest in building had been aroused and was to grow rapidly, he still spent much of his time preparing projects to put before the Royal Society. When King Charles decided to visit Gresham College, Lord Brouncker, the president, wrote to Christopher in Oxford to ask him to devise a program that would amuse the King. Christopher gave this a great deal of thought. It was no good being so learned that the King would not understand what they were talking about, and yet, he felt, there must be something of pomp. There are plenty of fairly simple scientific experiments that are so spectacular as almost to rank as conjuring tricks—"Knacks," he calls them, and "things to raise wonder such as even jugglers abound with"—but demonstrations of that kind would "scarce become the Gravity of the Occasion." It was necessary to find a happy medium, something "whose Use and Advantage is obvious, and without a lecture: and besides may surprise with some unexpected Effect and be commendable for Ingenuity of the Contrivance." Half a dozen experiments of this sort, he considered, would be enough for an hour's entertainment, and he felt sure the Society could find six suitable subjects if they really tried. He himself, he wrote, had nothing by him at the moment that would do. This is surprising; Christopher was seldom at a loss, and when it came to entertaining the King, one would have thought he could have come up with something new and interesting. This time, however, he offers little but advice.

> Experiments in Anatomy, though of the most value for their Use, are sordid and noisome to any but those whose Desire of Knowledge makes them digest it. Experiments for the Establishment of Natural Philosophy are seldom pompous. It is upon Billiards and Tennis Balls; upon the purling of Sticks and Tops, upon a Vial of Water or Wedge of Glass . . .

In despair, he seems to be falling back on "Knacks." But he ends his letter with a few suggestions that were probably adopted. He lists a weather wheel that automatically records meteorological changes; an artificial eye at least as large as a tennis ball; and a compass to guide travelers by coach, the vibration caused by the roughness of the road compensated for by an elaborate system of springs. This was an invention of his own. He also suggests that, if a little window were cut in the floor of the coach, the traveler might keep himself amused by consulting a "way-wiser," his boyhood invention for measuring distances traveled, which would be "fixed to the pearch." One's own practical mind suggests that the way-wiser would soon have been coated with mud—but Kit Wren had probably thought of a way around that difficulty too.

It seems at first sight strange that Christopher should not have been present at the meeting that the King was to attend. But he had, in fact, strained the patience of the university authorities almost to the breaking point with his prolonged absences in London. A letter from his great friend Dr. Sprat in Oxford, playfully written though it was, showed the way the wind blew.

My Dear Sir,

I must confess I have some little Peek against you: therefore am not much displeased that I have the occasion of telling you some ill news. The Vice Chancellor did yesterday send for me, to enquire where the Astronomy Professor was, and the Reason of his Absense so long after the Begining of the Term. I used all the arguments I could for your defense. I told him, that Charles the Second was King of England, Scotland, France and Ireland; that he was, by the last Act of Parliament, declared absolute Monarch in these his Dominions; and that it was this Mighty Prince who had confined you to London. I endeavoured to persuade him that the Drawing of Lines in Sir Harry Saville's School was not altogether of so great a Concernment for the Benefit of Christendom as the Rebuilding of St. Paul's or the Fortifying of Tangier: for I understood those were the great Works in which that extraordinary Genius of yours was judged necessary to be employed. All this I urged, but after some discourse . . . he most terribly told me, that he took it very ill that you had not all this while given him any Account what hindered you from the Discharge of your Office. This he bid me tell you and I do it not very unwillingly, because I see that our Friendships are so closely tied together, that the same Thing which was so great a Prejudice to me (my losing your Company all this while here) does also something redound to your Disadvantage. And so, my dear sir, now my Spite and Spleen are satisfied, I must needs return to my old Temper again, and faithfully assure you, that I am, with the most violent Zeal and Passion,

Your most affectionate,
and devoted Servant,
THOMAS SPRAT

Back went Christopher to Oxford, where, in addition to his duties as Professor of Astronomy, he occupied himself, in company with Dr. Wallis, on improving the telescope and practicing his skill as an engraver, which he had first taught himself as a boy. He became so good at it that he was given credit for the invention of a process known as mezzotint—but this was one thing that he did not invent. The real inventor was a German Army officer, who confided the secret to Prince Rupert, who demonstrated it to the Royal Society, where it was seen by Christopher, who used the method for his illustrations for Dr. Willis's book, *Anatomy of the Brain.* Engraving is a slow, laborious job, and although Christopher found it useful to reproduce detailed drawings, he could not spare the time to do very much of it.

The next assignment for Christopher as an architect was from the University of Oxford, and it was to design a block of students' rooms for Trinity College. He drew the plans and then left the work in the hands of a builder called Minchin, who came from Bletchington and had therefore probably been known to Christopher since his days at the rectory.

Minchin was left in charge while Christopher, for the first and only time in his life, went abroad. He was off to Paris, at the invitation of the British ambassador, the Earl of St. Albans. Since it was summer and the time of the long vacation, he could leave Oxford with a clear conscience, looking forward eagerly to studying French architecture and widening his knowledge of building. In any event, he stayed away from home for six months. And if when he left England he was more astronomer than architect, when he returned he was undoubtedly more architect than astronomer. Six months' study of other men's work kindled in him a desire to excel in this new field of endeavor.

7

A Visit to Paris

THE LONDON that Christopher Wren left in the summer of 1665 was a city that had progressed very little since the Middle Ages. Much of it was unbelievably squalid. Although the rich lived in handsome brick or stone houses, the vast majority of the citizens huddled together in dwellings of lath and tar and plaster. Thatched roofs were a commonplace, sanitation was practically unknown, refuse was simply thrown out of the window, rats bred and multiplied. Streets were narrow and traffic jams frequent, as huge wagons, rich men's carriages, horse riders, and tradesmen's carts jostled and rattled over the cobblestones. Foot passengers had a dangerous time. What often saved them from being crushed under the wheels of traffic were stout posts set up at the sides of the street, behind which they could find a precarious safety—if they cared to risk being deluged with dirty water thrown out of a window above.

Under such conditions, disease was rampant. Several times the city had suffered outbreaks of bubonic plague—known as the Black Death—but never had there been an epidemic of such proportions as the one that struck in 1665.

It was heralded, so people believed, by the appearance of a comet that was first seen on Christmas Eve of the previous year. Samuel Pepys went out into the street to see it, and noted in his diary that it passed so near the houses that many people considered it "imparted something very peculiar to the City alone." The King watched it from the window of his closet with superstitious unease. He believed in signs and portents and he feared that this strange "star" might be a warning of disaster. Christopher, who at that time was particularly interested in comets, no doubt observed it with scientific detachment, and wrote a paper on the subject which was read to the Royal Society. Whether he, too, believed in "signs and portents" is doubtful. The people who did believe must have felt themselves justified when, with the coming of summer, plague once again descended on their city.

It was a hot, dry summer, perfect breeding weather for a contagious disease. In the streets, decaying refuse smelled to high heaven, and the big, black, plague-carrying rats crept in and out of the insanitary houses, a living trail of destruction and hideous death.

At first, no one was particularly alarmed. Hot weather always brought a few cases of plague, always had, always would. And when thirty or forty people were packed together in a three-room house, how could anyone stop the contagion from spreading? The best one could do was to close the house where a death had occurred and keep the rest of the inhabitants prisoner until the quarantine period was over. Of course it was hard luck on these people. Imprisoned in the dark, airless, stinking house, they were almost sure to sicken and die too, but what else was there to do? So, paint a cross on the door, set a guard on the house, and hope the disease would be contained.

This time, however, these inhumane precautions were not enough to stop the spread of the infection. It ran like wildfire through the filthy streets, where for weeks not even a shower of rain had fallen to wash some of the refuse into the gutters and, finally, into the Thames. Pedestrians picked their way through the filth, a scented handkerchief or a bunch of herbs held to their noses; some plugged their nostrils with pellets of wormwood and breathed through their mouths. Rich men sent wives and children away to their country estates and presently, in a panic, themselves followed. Business in the city almost ground to a halt. By midsummer London was in the grip of the most appalling outbreak of plague that had ever occurred or was ever to occur again.

It was from this stricken city that Christopher took his departure and crossed to France. There was no question of a panic flight in his case—he could have stayed safely in Oxford if he had wished—but the visit to Paris had been long planned. The fact that Gresham House was closed and the Royal Society meetings canceled until happier times only confirmed him in his intention to enlarge his horizons by visiting a foreign country. He had never been abroad before.

He was fortunate in being the guest of so important a person as the British ambassador. Lord St. Albans was a great friend of Charles II's mother, Queen Henrietta Maria; in fact, some people believed that he was privately married to her. Whether this was so or not, he was certainly very much the courtier, and he knew all the architects, sculptors, and painters who thronged the court of Louis XIV, himself a great patron of the arts. St. Albans was not at all the type of man with whom the sober and industrious Christopher would normally have made friends. He was a gambler, a plotter, and he loved good living, but he also loved beautiful things and he was influential. It was as a patron that Christopher valued him, and he certainly smoothed the path of the budding architect in the French capital.

It was a Dr. Bateman to whom Christopher owed his introduction to the British ambassador, and after a while Christopher wrote to thank him for his help and to tell him of his doings in Paris.

> I have busied myself in surveying the most esteemed Fabrick of Paris and the Country round: the Louvre for a while was my daily object where no less than a thousand hands are constantly employed in the Works, some in laying mighty Foundations, some in raising the Stories, Columns, Entablements etc. with vast stones by great and useful Engines; others in Carving, Inlaying of Marbles, Plaistering, Painting, Gilding etc. which altogether make

a School of Architecture the best, probably of this day in Europe.

Christopher's horizons were widening. His future work was to owe a great deal to what he learned in France.

His stay in Paris lasted longer than, one imagines, was originally intended. It seems likely that at first he had only meant to spend the long vacation there, returning to his duties at Oxford at the beginning of the autumn term. After the strong hints thrown out by the chancellor of the university about his too frequent absences in London, even when he was on the King's business, one wonders that he should have felt free to stay abroad right through the winter—but this he did. It was March of the following year before Oxford saw him again, and by that time the plague had taken its appalling toll (nearly seventy thousand deaths were recorded in the City alone, and many more went unrecorded) and London was struggling back to normality—unaware that another catastrophe was shortly to befall it.

Across the channel, however, Dr. Christopher Wren, with his usual single-mindedness and his extraordinary powers of concentration, was utterly absorbed in the study of architecture and was in addition having a very good time.

An Academy of Painters, Sculpters, Architects and the chief Artificers of the Louvre meet every first and last Saturday of the Month. Mons. Colbert, Surintendant, comes to the works of the Louvre every Wednesday, and, if Busi-

> ness hinders not, Thursday. The Workmen are paid every Sunday duly. Mons. Abbé Charles introduced me to the Acquaintance of Bernini who showed me his Design of the Louvre and of the King's Statue.

Bernini was an Italian from Rome who had been brought to Paris by King Louis to submit plans for part of the Louvre. He was given very special treatment on entering France, but all the same, by the time he reached Paris, he found that a design by a Frenchman, Claude Perrault, was being considered. That design was finally chosen. The Italian was affronted, feeling that he had made his journey for nothing. But the King soothed him by giving him a handsome pension and a commission to execute a statue.

Christopher's letter goes on:

> . . . the Design of the Louvre I would have given my skin for, but the old, reserved Italian give me but a few Minutes View; it was five little designs in Paper, for which he hath received as many thousand Pistoles: I had only time to copy it in my Fancy and Memory: I shall be able by Discourse and a Crayon, to give you a tolerable Account of it.

It was the Louvre, that great palace on the banks of the Seine, which most captured Christopher's imagination. Churches, which later he was to make so particularly his own, took second place in his interest at this time. It was palaces, châteaux, and great gardens which intrigued him. He did, however, pay a great deal of attention to domes. There were many domed churches in France, and Bernini may well have discussed with him the construction of domes, which were a feature of Italian architecture. Christopher loved domes, and we have only to look at St. Paul's Cathedral to see what good use he made of the knowledge he gained in France.

The busy, happy days passed rapidly. Christopher visited Versailles, where the famous architect Mansard was hard at work remodeling the great château begun by Louis XIII. He had had 36,000 workmen and 6,000 horses working on the project, in order to have the place ready for a great fete held the year before, and work was still going on. Christopher was not particularly impressed. He found the decorations garish; his taste lay in simpler things. "The palace [of Versailles] called me twice to view it," he writes. "The mixtures of Brick, Stone, blue tile and gold make it look like a rich livery. Not an inch within but is crowned with little Curiousities of Ornaments."

Fontainebleau he visited too, commenting that it had "a stately Wilderness and Vastness suitable to the Desert it stands in." He follows this with a list of fourteen other châteaux he surveyed, of which he particularly liked Vaux, at Melun, not far from Paris. Vaux had been built in 1653, with a central dome, and there are certain features of it which suggest that Christopher may have had it in mind when completing the exterior of the Sheldonian. Certainly, the French influence can be traced in much of his work after this trip abroad.

But all good things come to an end, and by February 1666 he knew the time had come to go home. Perhaps pressure was being put upon him by the university, which would hardly be surprising. Perhaps, as he hints, money was running short. He wrote to a friend:

> I hope I shall give you a very good account of all the best Artists in France, my Business now is to pry into Trades and Arts. I put myself into all Shapes, to humour them: it is a Comedy to me and although sometimes expenseful I am loth to leave it . . . My Lord Berkeley returns to England at Christmas and I propose to take the opportunity of his Company, and by that time to perfect what I have on the Anvil—Observations on the present State of Architecture, Art and Manufactures in France.

Lord Berkeley, a member of the Royal Society, either delayed his journey or traveled alone, for Christopher did not arrive back in London until the end of February 1666. The prolonged absence from his own country undoubtedly marked a turning point in his life. Although he still held his professorship for some years, astronomy now took second place in his interests. His powerful mind and imagination were set on architecture, stimulated by what he had seen and studied in France and been told of Italy. What the French could do, the English could do better, may well have been his conviction, and he set to work immediately to prove it. By the first of May he put his report on the condition of St. Paul's, made at the request of the Dean and Chapter, before King Charles. His long association with the cathedral had now really begun.

Part III

"HIS MAJESTIE'S SURVEYOR OF WORKS"

. . . I must afirm, that since the time of Archimedes, there scarce ever met in one man, in so great a perfection, such a mechanical hand and so philosophical a mind.

ROBERT HOOKE

8

The Great Fire

CHRISTOPHER WREN had no sooner arrived back in England than he set to work on his report concerning the renovation of St. Paul's. The whole scheme had been put aside during the months of the plague, when men had other things to think about than the restoration of old buildings. But now the epidemic was over, except for a few cases in the "Liberties," as the teeming areas outside the walls of the City were called. The capital was slowly returning to a normal way of life, the rich reopened their town houses, and the coaches that had carried panic-stricken wives and families into the purer air of the country now rattled over the cobblestones again and turned in at the high gates of the great houses whose gardens ran down to the Thames. The King was back at St. James's Palace, shops reopened, and life, for the survivors, began again. Only the wig-makers still found trade slow. For a long time, men of fashion hesitated to buy a new wig, in case the hair should have been taken from the head of a plague victim—a grizzly thought, but not without foundation. Slowly, dogs and cats—which had all been slaughtered during the worst days of the epidemic, lest they carry the infection—began to appear once again in the streets.

On February 21, Gresham College reopened, and the weekly meetings of the Royal Society began again. Mr. Samuel Pepys went to the first meeting and reported in his diary that Dr. Jonathan Goddard, the Professor of Physics, "did fill us with talk, in defence of his and his fellow physicians going out of town in plague-time; saying that their particular patients were most gone out of town and they left at liberty, and a great deal more . . ." Pepys expresses the contempt of the man who stayed for the man who fled, and certainly it would seem a terrible thing that doctors left at such a time, on the slender excuse that their own patients—the rich—had gone, leaving them nothing to do.

The Royal Society debated the whole wretched affair of the plague, earnestly seeking methods of preventing such an outbreak again. Many ways of improving conditions must have occurred to them. Clearly, anyone who could keep his house sanitary and free from rats had a better chance of survival. But the problem was on a national rather than a domestic scale. Extensive reconstruction was long overdue, and it took the Great Fire, just as three hundred years later it took the German blitz, to wipe out at least some of the slums and give the authorities a chance to begin again.

The deplorable state of St. Paul's Cathedral had been apparent long before the year of the Great Plague. Cromwell's troops, who had turned the nave into a cavalry barracks, torn down scaffolding and removed many of the materials introduced by Inigo Jones in the years before the war, only completed the ruin into which the great church had been allowed to fall. Christopher discounted the damage done by the troops and put most of the blame on the thirteenth-century masons who built the cathedral—which hardly seems fair, seeing that the roof they built had stood for four centuries. He did not like Gothic architecture, and in his eyes nothing Gothic was good. In his report, he wrote:

> First, it is evident by the Ruin of the Roof, that the Work was both ill-designed and ill-Built from the Beginning: ill-designed, because the Architect gave not Butment enough to counterpoise, and resist the weight of the Roof from spreading the Walls; for, the Eye alone will discover to any Man, that those Pillars as vast as they are, even eleven foot diameter, are bent outwards at least six inches from their first position . . .

The report was long and detailed and very startling to the Dean and Chapter, who had not realized what a dangerous state the cathedral was in, or how much trouble and expense would be involved in putting it to rights.

A meeting was called to discuss the problem. The Bishop of London was there, and the Dean of St. Paul's, Sir John Evelyn, and various other interested people, together with Christopher Wren. The company was divided in its opinions—some agreeing with Christopher that the walls were being pushed outward by the weight of the roof, others contending that the sloping walls were deliberate "for an Effect in Perspective in Regard of the

Height." The argument raged for some time, and the only point on which they all agreed was that they would like to have a "noble Cupola," or dome. This, they said, was "a form of Church building not as yet known in England, but of wonderful grace; for this purpose we offered to bring in a Plan and Estimate, which after much Contest was at last assented to, and that we should nominate a Committee of able Workmen to examine the present Foundation."

They might have saved themselves the trouble. Five days after Evelyn reported this meeting in his diary, on September 2, 1666, the Great Fire of London broke out. By the time it was finally quenched, St. Paul's Cathedral was a shattered, blackened ruin in the midst of a shattered and blackened city.

IT WAS JUST BEFORE MIDNIGHT on Saturday, September 1, that the King's baker, Thomas Farynor, and his daughter Hannah went to bed in their house in Pudding Lane. The house was an old, wooden-frame one in a closely packed street of similar houses. Downstairs were piled faggots and brushwood to heat the bread ovens, and in the early hours of Sunday morning, fire started in the pile. How it started is unknown. Every explanation has been put forward, including a farfetched story of a Popish plot, which gained such credence that eventually a poor half-witted boy was hanged for the crime. It seems more

SIR CHR: WREN.
Late Surveyor General of
the Royal Buildings.

Courtesy The National Portrait Gallery, London

Kneller's portrait of Sir Christopher Wren (1711)

Courtesy The Guildhall Library, London

An artist's rendering of the upper ward of Windsor Castle

Courtesy The National Portrait Gallery, London

Nanteuil's portrait of Sir John Evelyn

The New York Public Library Picture Collection

Sir Christopher Wren's first design for St. Paul's

Courtesy The National Portrait Gallery, London

J. M. Wright's portrait of King Charles II

The New York Public Library Picture Collection

Wren's Great Model of St. Paul's, executed in wood

The New York Public Library Picture Collection

The Monument, London, commemorating the great fire of 1666

The New York Public Library Picture Collection

An example of the fine carving of Grinling Gibbons, on the altarpiece of St. James's Church, London

likely that a spark flew out from the kitchen hearth, or hot ashes were scattered by a draft. Whatever the cause, the result was devastating. Two hours after going to bed, Thomas, Hannah, and their two servants were wakened to find the house aflame, with thick clouds of smoke billowing up the stairs. There was no hope of getting down; the only way of escape was by the roof. Three of them scrambled out and crept over the tiles to the house next door. But the maidservant was more afraid of heights than of the fire. She stayed behind, and her screams ceased abruptly as the roof collapsed in a roar of flames. Hers was the first life to be lost in the terror that ensued.

A house on fire was nothing unusual in the London of those days; it happened all the time. At first it seemed that the fire in Pudding Lane was of small consequence. But there were several things about this particular fire that made it tragically different from any other.

To begin with, the location helped make it a torch that kindled the city. Pudding Lane was a double row of tumble-down, wooden-frame houses leaning toward one another across a narrow, dark, cobblestoned street. The house walls had been weatherproofed with a coating of pitch, and this, after the long, hot summer was peeling off in hard, black flakes. The lane ran down to the Thames, and on the banks of the river, warehouses clustered around the wharves, packed with casks of oil, pitch, tar, cases of sugar and butter, and leather for the Cordwainers' Company. Stocks of timber and coal brought by barge up the river were piled on the wharves. And toward this gigantic potential bonfire the Pudding Lane flames crept, slowly but inexorably.

The second thing that contributed to the severity of the fire was the weather. The summer had been hot and dry, and now a keen wind was blowing from the northeast. The scene was set for destruction, but the players, the citizens of London, were curiously slow to appreciate their danger. Although the Lord Mayor, Sir Thomas Bludworth, was called at 3 A.M. and arrived at the scene of the fire with some of his city officers shortly afterward, he refused to take the matter seriously and was peevish at having been disturbed. The fire, he said crossly, would burn itself out. And he went back to bed.

Samuel Pepys took much the same view. In his diary, he wrote:

> Jane [his maid] called us up at about three in the morning to tell us of a great fire they saw in the City. So I rose, and slipped on my nightgown, and went to the window, and thought it to be on the back-side of Marke Lane at the farthest, but being unused to such fires as followed, I thought it far enough off: and so went to bed again and to sleep.

It was the last sound sleep he had for several nights to come. By the time the truth of the situation came home to the authorities, the fire, aided by the wind, had gained a firm hold and was beyond control.

Now began four days of indescribable chaos. Perhaps if there had been organized and intelligent control right from the start, the damage might not have been so great. But one has to remember the difficulty of communications in those times. Messages from one authority to another had to be sent by hand. The streets, many of them impassable because of collapsed and burning houses, were further blocked by people frantically endeavoring to remove themselves and their household goods by wagon, cart, hand barrow, or pack horse. The very cobblestones grew so hot that men's boots were burned off their feet, horses panicked and bolted. And still the wind blew strongly from the east. Fire paths were made by pulling down buildings with great iron hooks. These, attached to ropes, were thrown up to engage in the upper part of the house and then teams of men and horses dragged on the ropes until the whole front fell away, exposing the interior like a doll's house when the door is opened. Then the hooks were once again thrown up and the rest of the house crashed in ruins to the ground. It was no use. The fire leaped the narrow gaps without pausing in its terrible advance. Later, gunpowder was used to blast wider paths, and this had more success. But by the time permission was given to bring the powder from the magazine in the Tower, it was too late to save St. Paul's.

The fire reached the cathedral on the third day. So convinced had the shopkeepers in the neighborhood been of the invulnerability of the huge stone building that they had removed their goods to what they believed was the safety of the crypt. There, below the ground, were stacked articles of gold and silver, valuable bales of silks and velvets, and books, especially books, for St. Paul's Churchyard, as the area around the cathedral was called, was the great center for booksellers, and valuable books, worth, some said, at least £150,000 were stacked in the crypt. In all, a quarter of a million pounds' worth of goods had been taken to St. Paul's for safety. Not £250 worth survived the flames.

The fire approached the great church from every quarter of the compass. At first it seemed to the anxious watchers that, by a miracle, the cathedral might be spared, for the huge roof rose out of the smoke, seemingly unharmed. But shortly before dusk some planks that had been laid across a gap where the lead had broken away caught alight, and when darkness fell, St. Paul's was a mass of flames. An observer wrote:

> The church, though all of stone outward, though naked of houses about it, and though so high above all buildings in the City, yet within a while doth yield to the violent assaults of the conquering flames, and strongely takes Fire at the top; now the Lead melts and runs down, as if it had been snow before the sun; and the great beams and mossy stones, with a great noise, fall upon the Pavement, and break through into Faith Church underneath; now great flakes of stone scale, and peel off strongely from the side of the walls.

St. Faith's was really a church within a church. It was part of the crypt of St. Paul's and had been adopted by the booksellers and stationers as their own special church. It was in St. Faith's that the great store of books met their end, when the cathedral roof—made of timber, with a protecting "skin" of lead—crashed through the building, carrying with it a thousand tons of stone. The heat from the burning timber and the molten sea of lead was so great that the outer walls split, and enormous chunks of stone, like giant shrapnel, flew into the surrounding streets. "The stones of Paul's flew like granados," wrote Evelyn, "the Lead melting downe the streetes in a streame, and the very pavements of them glowing with firey redresse, so as nor horse nor man was able to tread on them."

The books in the crypt burned for a week and the wind scattered the charred pages for miles, a dismal reminder of irretrievable loss. Some of the scorched paper fell among the 150,000 homeless people camping in the fields to the north of the city, crouching in tents made from bed hangings and blankets, and facing a grim future as they watched their past lives go up in flames and smoke.

On the fourth day the wind changed, blowing softly from the west, and the fire began to die. By Friday the ground had cooled sufficiently to allow Sir John Evelyn to make his way through the City and stand before the pitiful ruin of the great church he loved so well. "I was," he says, "infinitely concerned to find the goodly Church of St. Paules now a sad Ruin and that beautiful Portico . . . now rent in pieces. Flakes of vast stones split asunder and nothing remaining entire but the Inscription on the Architrave showing by whom it was built, which had not one letter of it defaced . . . Thus lay in ashes that most venerable Church . . . besides neere 100 more."

Christopher Wren was not long behind him. He too surveyed the ruins with sorrow, but also perhaps with a rising hope that out of the ashes might grow an even nobler edifice, and that the guiding hand might be his own.

9

The Surveyor-General

THE FIRE had scarcely died down when Christopher was already hard at work drawing up plans for a new City of London. It was a tremendous opportunity to set right so many things that had made the old City inconvenient; it was an architect's dream, and Christopher was now a dedicated architect. Nor was he the only one to turn all his energies to the planning of a new city. Sir John Evelyn also drew up plans, which he submitted to the King on September 13, a week after the fire was over. But Christopher was before him. "Dr Wren got the start of me," comments Evelyn in a letter to a friend. It is quite possible that neither of them knew the other was engaged on the same work. Certainly the fact that they were rivals made no difference to their friendship.

King Charles studied both schemes with care. Had he been a dictator with absolute power, had he been prepared to turn a blind eye to the inconvenience and suffering of the people of London, had he thought of nothing but building up an ideal city, then either of the schemes would have been of great interest to him. But they were, he realized, dreams, not practicalities. To carry out these schemes, it would have been necessary to ride roughshod over private ownership, leaseholds, and tenancies. It would have been necessary to find accommodations for an unspecified time for thousands of homeless people, and to have interfered gravely with business and trade. Moreover, both Evelyn and Wren proposed such drastic changes that public sentiment would have been outraged. What? Move the Royal Exchange to Thames-side? But the Royal Exchange has *always* stood in the heart of the City! What! Move the halls of the City Companies? Impossible! The King understood the minds of his subjects better than did the planners. Reluctantly, he rejected both Utopian schemes. London must be rebuilt as quickly as possible, and this meant compromise all along the line. Many improvements could undoubtedly be made, but public buildings must, as far as possible, be left on their old sites, and private ownership of land must be respected.

Christopher was disappointed. An opportunity to build an ideal city must be every planner's dream. But he was, as usual, philosophical, and set to work once again to draw up plans that were workable. It was an incredibly complicated task. Streets must be widened—everyone was agreed on that. But to take more land for streets meant that someone had to give up part of his frontage, and then he would be entitled to compensation. The old, wooden-frame houses must be replaced by houses of brick and stone. The occupants must decide whether they could afford a two-, three-, or four-story house, for the streets would be laid out in terraces, all the houses alike. Sewers must be put in; it was a unique opportunity to do something drastic to clean up the horrible sanitary conditions and improve the health of the people. Looking back, what surprises us now is not that the new city was far from ideal but that it was not far worse. The man London had to thank for this was, first and foremost, Dr. Christopher Wren.

In the state of emergency that existed, Christopher was appointed Surveyor-General in place of Sir John Denham, who, already in poor health, had suffered family troubles and had become mentally ill. The appointment was not made official for another three years, as, while Sir John lived, the King did not wish to take the post from him. In any event, Sir John gave it up voluntarily to Christopher in 1669, and died shortly afterward.

But now, in the year 1666, with London in smoking ruins, a capable man had to be set in supreme command, and Christopher was the chosen man. He was appointed Principal Architect for "repairing the whole City, the Cathedral church of St. Paul's, all the parochial Churches with other Public Structures."

How did Christopher feel when he found himself the key figure in this colossal project? He had done very little actual building. He was still, by profession, a teacher of astronomy. As always, he was a little diffident about undertaking new work—and now he was thrust into a position of enormous importance. Thousands of people would be dependent upon him for a speedy return to normal life in homes of their own, and his was the responsibility to posterity to fashion a city worthy to be the capital of a great and rapidly expanding country. It was a responsibility anyone might have shrunk from, but there is no evidence that Christopher, still quite a young man, hesitated this time to shoulder the burden. Of course he had many excellent friends and helpers. He was not alone, but he was the head of the team. He was a modest man, not overconfident and never overbearing, but he must have had the inner conviction of his own ability that comes to men of genius.

His first task was to survey the damage to St. Paul's and send in a report to the King, and this he proceeded to do with his customary thoroughness. It was absolutely clear to him that the repairs planned before the fire were now out of the question, the damage was far too great, and almost total rebuilding was, in his opinion, necessary. The Dean and Chapter, however, faced with this enormous expense, indulged in wishful thinking and still clung to their opinion that the original repairs, plus, perhaps, a little extra building, would do. In the meantime, they urgently wanted part of the cathedral to be made usable, so that services could again be held. Christopher agreed that this could be done, and after careful consideration he put forward an acceptable plan for interim repairs, using, as far as possible, materials salvaged from the fire. In his report, he wrote:

> Having with this ease obtained a present Cathedral, there will be time to consider of a more durable and noble Fabrick, to be made in the Tower and Eastern parts of the

> Church, when the minds of men, now contracted to many objects of necessary Charge, shall by God's blessing be more widened, after a happy restoration both of the Buildings and Wealth of the City and Nation. In the meanwhile to derive, if not a stream, yet some little drills of Charitie this way, or at least to preserve that already obtained from being diverted, it may not prove ill advised to seem to begin something of this new Fabrick.

This was cunning of Christopher. He knew very well that, with so many of the rich and influential citizens absorbed in rebuilding their own homes and businesses, it was hardly the time to try to raise funds for a gigantic undertaking such as the rebuilding of the cathedral. On the other hand, if nothing at all was done until times improved, people might lose interest altogether, and the church funds, such as they were, might be diverted to some other, more pressing need. Nearly one hundred parish churches had been lost in the flames and the parishioners might feel that the funds of the cathedral church, if not needed immediately, could well be spent on raising up their local place of worship.

The King agreed with Christopher. Four months after the fire, he issued an order for the work to begin.

> *Jan 15th 1667, at Whitehall*
>
> Whereas the dreadfull Calamity of Fire . . . hath in particular fallen so heavily upon the Cathedral Church of St. Paul and . . . set back the Method of its Repairs we cannot . . . hope suddenly to proceed in that great Work. It being thought necessary in the mean Time (till it shall please God to bless us with a more favourable juncture for doing something more lasting and magnificent) that some

> part of the venerable Pile be forthwith restored to its religious use . . . it was this day ordered that a Choir and Auditory for present use be set out, repaired and finished in the Course of the next Summer in the Body of the Church between the West End and the second Pillars above the little North and South Dores.

The King, like the cathedral authorities, clung to the hope that the repairs planned before the fire could still be carried out, but Christopher kept his own opinion that nothing short of total rebuilding would be satisfactory in the long run. This, however, was not the moment to argue about it. He waited to see the start of the clearing up (an enormous job, since the streets surrounding the cathedral were still choked with rubble) and then went back to Oxford to resume his astronomy lectures and to see how the builders were getting on with the restorations at Trinity College and the completion of the Sheldonian Theatre. The rebuilding of the City was being ably and speedily dealt with by the committee under his leadership. Roger Pratt and Hugh May were both men with experience of architecture, as was Robert Hooke, then Professor of Mathematics at Gresham College, and Christopher's close friend. The three of them, together with a Mr. Germain, "an experienced man in buildings," and Mr. Milles, the City Surveyor, made up the committee. There is no doubt that at this time there were men among them, notably Pratt and May, who had reason to feel that they knew more about building than young Dr. Christopher Wren. They were good men at their job, and it must have been hard to have a professor of astronomy set over them. They would not have been human if they had not resented it. But with Christopher's attention divided by his other interests, they had things much in their own hands as far as the rebuilding of the City was concerned. Pratt had had hopes, quite well justified, that he might be appointed architect to St. Paul's, and had this happened, he would certainly have been a serious rival to Christopher Wren. But his life was destined to take a different course. A year after the fire, he inherited an estate in Norfolk. He then married a rich wife and retired, his last architectural work being to plan a house for himself in the country.

The three years from the time of the fire until Christopher's official appointment to the post of Surveyor-General were one of the busiest periods of his life. It was not until the early 1670's that he finally gave up his professorship, which must have taken up a fair portion of his time. In addition to this, he was head of the commission for the rebuilding of London, and architect for St. Paul's. He attended the meetings of the Royal Society fairly regularly in their new home at Arundel House, and this led to more work. Gresham College had been given over to the Mayor and Corporation, whose own premises were burned. And Arundel House, lent to the Society by Mr. Howard, later the Duke of Norfolk, was not really suitable for the Society, so they aspired to build themselves a permanent home. Mr. Howard presented them with a plot of land, and Robert Hooke, now Christopher's assistant, put forward a design. In doing this he "jumped the gun," because the Society wanted a Wren design and had already written to Christopher at Oxford asking him to go and see Mr. Howard, who was visiting the town, and put forward suggestions for the building. This Christopher did, and offered to make a model of the ambitious design he had in mind. But it was all too expensive, the funds could not be raised; there were legal difficulties too; and the college was never built.

Perhaps Christopher was glad not to have to take on this work. He was already working on a chapel for Emmanuel College, Cambridge, and a new Customs House in London. He also surveyed and reported on Salisbury Cathedral for his old friend Seth Ward, now Bishop of Salisbury. All this traveling around took time, and the inconvenience and discomfort of travel made it tiring for a man who, although healthy, had never been robust. If Christopher Wren had been what we describe nowadays as a "nervous type," he could never have got through his crowded days without a breakdown. It was his calmness, his refusal to allow things to get on top of him, his orderly mind, that stood him in such good stead. He was still a bachelor, so engrossed in his work that he seems to have had little time for social activities. At last, though, in 1669, the year he became Surveyor-General, he married. He was then thirty-seven years old.

The wife he chose was Faith Coghill, the daughter of Sir Thomas Coghill, Squire of Bletchington, and as Faith was only four years younger than himself, it is very likely that he had known her since he was a schoolboy living at the rectory with his sister and brother-in-law. It seems in keeping with his character that he should marry an old and tried friend, weighing the advantages of the match in his mind, taking his time before committing himself to such a change in life.

We know very little about Faith; it would be pleasant to know more. One small incident brings her to life for us. Shortly before the marriage, in December 1669, she "dunked" her watch accidentally in water, and—naturally—appealed to the versatile and practical Christopher to put it right.

Christopher found the damage beyond his powers and took it to a watch repairer, who kept it for a long time. At last it was returned, and Christopher packed it carefully and sent it back to Faith with a letter. The letter is very much a product of its time. It is, by our standards, flowery and a little insincere. It might have been written to a child rather than to a mature woman of thirty-three, but still, when people are in love they often write and talk to one another in a language of their own. They have secret jokes which no outsider can understand. So here is a small mystery which can never be solved. Was the sober bachelor at long last in love, or did he just write this charming letter in the fashion of the day?

> *Madam,* The Artificer having never before met with a drowned watch, like an ignorant physician has been so long about the cure that he hath made me very unquiet that your commands should be so long deferred; however, I have sent the watch at last and envy the felicity of it, that it should be so near your side and so often enjoy your eye

and be consulted by you how your time shall pass while you employ your hand in your excellent works. But have a care of it for I put a spell into it that every beating of the balance will tell you 'tis the pulse of my heart which labours as much to serve you and more truly than the watch; for the watch I believe will sometimes lie, and sometimes be idle and unwilling to go, having received so much injury by being drenched in that briny bath, that I despair it should ever be a true servant to you more. But as for me (unless you drown me too in my tears) you may be confident I shall never cease to be

Your most Affectionate, humble Servant,
CHRISTOPHER WREN

Postscript. I have put the watch in a box that it might take no harme, and wrapt it about with a little Leather, and that it might not jog, I was fain to fill up the corners with either a few shavings or waste paper.

The postscript is pure Wren, the practical, painstaking man, as much concerned with the safe packing of a watch as with the designing of St. Paul's. But poor Faith had only five years left in which to wear her watch. On September 4, 1675, after an illness of eleven days, she died of smallpox, leaving Christopher with a little son, seven months old. Her first child, whom they christened Gilbert, had died in infancy the year before, but the new baby was strong and seemed likely to live even without his mother's care. He was called Christopher after his father and grandfather and he grew up to follow in his father's footsteps and become his assistant. It was he who collected the material for a history of the Wren family which is called

Parentalia and which was published by his own son, Stephen.

But all this is in the future. The year is 1669. Christopher is at last, by courtesy of old Sir John Denham, Surveyor-General and has taken his bride to the house which "went with the job," a very grand London house in Scotland Yard, part of the King's palace of Whitehall. Here also was housed the Office of Works, of which Christopher was now the head.

The position of Surveyor-General was the highest open to an architect at that time. Christopher owed the honor directly to the personal interest of King Charles II, and that interest had first been aroused by the drawings of insects presented to him by the brilliant young member of the Royal Society. One wonders if, without those insects, St. Paul's Cathedral might have been designed by another hand and the famous dome never made to rise above the roofs of London. There was a good deal of feeling in some quarters about Christopher's appointment, but no open enmity. He was too well liked, and the quality of his brain was too widely recognized and appreciated for that. One or two men who felt that they had been unfairly passed over had a private moan, especially Hugh May, Comptroller of the Office of Works, who complained bitterly about the matter to Mr. Samuel Pepys.

With the beginning of the 1670's, with his new position, his new home, and his new wife, Christopher Wren's life enters a new phase. He is now all architect, although he still retains his keen interest in astronomy and the other sciences and is an active member of the Royal Society. For another three years he held the Savillian Professorship, though how he managed to carry out his duties in Oxford, one cannot imagine. Possibly he found someone to act as his deputy. He could afford to do so now, with his reasonable though not magnificent salary as Surveyor-General.

In 1670 something happened which affected Christopher's work. The King passed the Rebuilding Act, and more money was allocated for the new St. Paul's. Most of this money was raised by putting a higher tax on coal. Money was urgently needed, for Christopher had been proved right about the impossibility of patching up the ruins left by the fire. It had been tried, with disastrous results. The Dean wrote to Christopher while he was still at Oxford, and Christopher would not have been human if he had not felt pleased, after having had his advice set aside. Wrote the Dean:

> *Sir* . . . What you whispered in my ear at your last coming hither, is now come to pass. Our Work at the West-end of St Paul's is fallen about our ears. Your quick Eye discerned the Walls and Pillars gone off from their Perpendiculars and I believe other Defects too, which are now exposed to every common Observer.

It is always pleasant to be right, and it was especially satisfactory for Christopher because he cared deeply about St. Paul's. He had been disappointed and hurt when his advice was rejected and it seemed that the cathedral church of London was to be all botched up. But now everything was going right—he was given a free hand. When he asked the Dean to tell him how much money would be available so that he might fit his plans to the finances, he was told, quite indignantly, to draw up suitable plans without taking money into account. His instructions were to "frame a Design handsome and noble, and suitable to all the ends of it, and to the Reputation of the City, and the Nation, and to take it for granted, that Money will be had to accomplish it."

The scene was set. The new Surveyor-General plunged heart and soul into the gigantic task before him, happy in the knowledge that he had the trust of the authorities and an unlimited sum of money behind him.

In 1673 the King conferred a knighthood on the man whom he liked personally and valued for his great ability. The big house in Scotland Yard was now the home of Sir Christopher and Lady Wren.

10

The Phoenix Years

WHAT SORT OF CITY was it which, like the Phoenix, rose from the ashes after the Great Fire? Rebuilding had begun almost before the ground cooled, and, as we have seen, good planning had to take second place to expediency. Many improvements were made, notably wider streets and more substantial buildings, but a golden opportunity to lay out a noble city was, inevitably, lost. Moreover, the teeming, stinking, overpopulated areas outside the walls of the old City had been untouched by the fire and were improved only gradually through the centuries to come.

The King's palace of Whitehall, St. James's Palace, and the area around were also untouched, the wind having changed just in time. It was the square mile known as the City that was wiped out, and in this square mile many homes and business premises had stood, and eighty-seven parish churches. The rebuilding of these churches was one of the undertakings assigned to Sir Christopher Wren.

Another task for the Surveyor-General was to turn a stream known as the Fleet Ditch into a canal leading to the Thames. This was a complicated engineering feat, very much after Sir Christopher's heart. He worked on it together with Robert Hooke and another architect called Oliver, but the canal was never a commercial success. It did not really seem to be needed, and it was covered over in 1773. Fleet Street, the street of newspapers, today lies over the Fleet Canal.

The redesigning of the City churches was a huge undertaking, even though, of the eighty-seven destroyed, only fifty-one were rebuilt. Quite a number of parishes combined in the newly planned areas—which must have been hard on the clergymen who lost their livings in consequence. Before a church could be rebuilt, the vicar and his churchwardens had to apply for a warrant, and when they had obtained this they took it to the Surveyor-General in his offices at Whitehall and asked him to draw up the plans. Then Sir Christopher would visit the site to see for himself how much ground the building could cover, and other practical matters. This visit was usually made a pleasant social occasion, when the churchwardens entertained the great man at dinner, or provided refreshments on the site. After that, the plans were drawn up and contracts made with masons, bricklayers, and carpenters. Multiply this performance by fifty-one and it is easy to see that Sir Christopher needed all the help he could get. The help was given by three City Surveyors—Hooke, Oliver, and a new man called Woodroffe. Sir Christopher, as far as we can discover, was responsible for the general design of all the churches, but the details he must surely have left to others on his staff.

Sir Christopher had an unusual problem to tackle in designing these churches. They not only had to look beautiful and be well built, they had to be adapted to a new form of worship. Few churches had been built in England in nearly two hundred years, and during that time the style of religious service had drastically changed. When the old Gothic churches had been built, the congregation played little part in the service, so the long chancels and side chapels, from which few people could catch even a glimpse of the altar, were quite suitable. The services were conducted in Latin, which only the educated few understood anyway, and for the common man it was enough that he was there. Participation, as we know it today, was not required. Now all that was changing. It was desirable that the congregation should be able to see and hear and join in the act of worship. Sir Christopher had to bear this in mind when designing the new buildings, and that he most brilliantly did. He was determined, too, that the churches not be alike. He wanted to add richness to the City by a diversity of architecture, some churches to bear a dome, some a spire, others a tower. Perhaps, in a way, the designing of these parish churches was to Sir Christopher a kind of rehearsal for the building of St. Paul's; perhaps he was feeling his way toward the ultimate design of the greatest of all his works.

It was during the time he was engaged on the City churches that Sir Christopher built the second model for St. Paul's. The first had been submitted soon after the Great Fire, when he was still tied to the idea of patching up what was left rather than rebuilding the whole. After the collapse of the walls, this early model was abandoned. Given a free hand at last, Sir Christopher now began to work on a second model. This is called the Great Model and can still be seen in the Trophy Room at St. Paul's. It is an enormous model, large enough to walk into and look around. It is made of wood, and cost the then huge sum of £600. Sir Christopher's son, in *Parentalia,* says it was made "to gratify the Connoiseurs and Criticks," but it also gratified the architect. He was extremely pleased with it, as well he may have been, and would have liked to build the cathedral to this design—but it was not altogether satisfactory to the King and the clergy. In the end, he had to modify it a good deal. Still, such a splendid model must have given great pleasure to Kit Wren the modelmaker, even though he was now too busy and too important a man to work on it himself. He had come a long way in the world since the happy, absorbed hours spent with pasteboard, colored inks, and glue.

After every major event in the history of a city or nation there comes the desire to commemorate it in a tangible way. This seems to be a universal urge, and the world is studded with monuments, statues, plaques, and memorial halls. London, it went without saying, must have a memorial to commemorate the Great Fire. So, in the midst of the urgent rebuilding of homes, offices, warehouses, and churches, the Surveyor-General and his team were required to design and build a reminder of the stupidity and incompetence that had led to the devastation of the City. Not that anybody thought of it in those terms, naturally. The hesitations and delay that turned what might have been a local fire into a catastrophe were conveniently forgotten. Many people believed that the whole thing had been a Popish plot; others believed it an act of God, sent to punish a wicked city for its sins.

The first point to be decided was the exact spot on which the memorial should stand. Sir John Evelyn felt the most appropriate place was where the fire stopped short so dramatically when the wind changed. The King, however, supported the faction that wanted the memorial built where the fire began, his chief reason being that this was a more central position. Accordingly, a site was chosen as near Pudding Lane as possible, and Sir Christopher and his devoted assistant Robert Hooke set to work to design a monument that would tower dramatically above the roofs of the City. Their first design was for an enormous single column with brazen flames bursting at intervals from the shaft. These flames were to be not only ornament but a device to hide the narrow windows that were necessary to light the interior, where a winding staircase led dizzily to the top of the column. There was an ulterior motive in this single-column design: Sir Christopher planned to use it in certain experiments for which the Royal Society had no suitable apparatus. But, although a modified form of his first design was built, the vibrations from the traffic in the street below interfered with the delicate mechanism needed for the experiments and made it useless. He had other frustrations as well. His idea was to set on the summit an enormous statue—of the King, or a symbolic figure of the City of London—but this was not approved. In the end, the great column was capped with a brass urn shooting forth flames. The column was 200 feet high and very much admired at the time. It was known, and is still known, as The Monument, and the energetic can climb the internal staircase and survey London from a narrow balcony near the top. It is not a great example of Wren architecture and one feels he must have looked on it as a necessary chore rather than a labor of love.

IT WAS IN FEBRUARY 1671 that Sir Christopher met a man whose genius, in his own line, equaled Wren's in his. He was dining with Sir John Evelyn and Mr. Samuel Pepys, the Clerk of the Acts, when he was shown a wood carving that he saw at once was a wonderful piece of work. He was excited by the possibility of having such an artist help in the decoration of his buildings and pressed Sir John to tell him where he had found the carving. The story was a strange one. He had been strolling, said Sir John Evelyn, around Deptford, near his own home, Sayes Court, when he happened to glance through the window of a "poore solitary thatched house," and there he saw a man absorbed in woodcarving. He came closer and saw with great surprise that the subject of the carving was derived from Tintoretto's *Crucifixion,* which he knew very well because, twenty-five years before, he had brought back a copy of it from Venice. It seemed strange to see such work being done in such a place, and he felt he must find out more about this man. Evelyn writes in his diary:

> I asked if I might enter; he opened the door civilly to me, and I saw about him such a work as for the curiousity of handling, drawing and studious exactness, I had never before seen in all my travels. I questioned him why he worked in such an obscure and lonesome place; he told me it was that he might apply himself to his profession without interruption, and wondered not a little how I found him out. I asked if he was unwilling to be made knowne to some great man, for that I believed it might turn to his profit: he answered he was yet a beginner, but would not be sorry to sell off that piece; on demanding the price, he said £100.

Now, a hundred pounds was a very large sum of money in those days, certainly a large price to be asked by a "beginner" for his work. But Evelyn was so struck with the quality of the piece that he was not at all put out.

> In good earnest, the very frame was worth the money, there being nothing in nature so tender and delicate as the flowers and festoons about it, and yet the work was very strong: in the piece were more than 100 figures of men etc. I found he was likewise musical, and very civil, sober and discreete in his discourse. So desiring leave to visit him sometimes, I went away.

This musical, civil, "discreete" young man who carved so beautifully was Grinling Gibbons, destined to be associated with Wren and other famous architects of his time, leaving his work in St. Paul's Cathedral and many other buildings to enrich our heritage.

Sir John Evelyn not only visited the young man again.

He introduced him and his work to the King, who was so delighted with one piece, a crucifix, that he took it with his own hands into the Queen's bedroom, thinking she might like to buy it, as she was a Catholic. And so she would have done, Evelyn notes resentfully, only the King was called away, and as soon as he had gone, "a French pedling woman . . . who used to bring peticoats and fans . . . began to find fault with several things in the worke, which she understood no more than an asse or a monkey, so in a kind of indignation I caused the person who brought it to carry it back to the chamber, finding the Queene so much governed by an ignorant French woman, and this incomparable artist had his labour only for his paines which not a little displeased me."

Whether the Queen bought this particular carving or not, however, the King now knew the genius of Grinling Gibbons, and he soon launched the young man on his successful career. Gibbons carved not only in wood but in marble, and later he made a bronze statue of King James II. Much of the work supposed to be by Gibbons was undoubtedly done by other hands: one man alone could not possibly have been responsible for everything that is attributed to him. But St. Paul's is certainly enriched by his work, both in wood and in stone, and some of the City churches as well. It was a lucky day for England, as well as for the artist himself, when Evelyn took that stroll through Deptford.

To be Surveyor-General of the Works was to be responsible not only for the rebuilding of London but for the upkeep and care of all buildings belonging to the Crown. This in itself was an enormous task. Sir Christopher was called upon to advise on a multitude of things. Even the decorations on royal occasions such as a wedding were his responsibility. He had under him a whole host of craftsmen. There was the master mason, the master carpenter, and the sergeant-plumber, each with his own workmen. There were bricklayers, joiners, plasterers, locksmiths, carvers, and a purveyor, who was responsible for buying all materials required. It was he who arranged for shipments of stone from the quarries of Dorsetshire and the Cotswold Hills, marble from Italy, fine timber from the New Forest in Hampshire and other places. Sailing barges brought most of the materials up the Thames to London, for the roads were bad, and heavy wagons drawn by teams of horses found it hard going even in summer and impossible when winter rains turned the roads into quagmires of mud. The most tiresome part of Sir Christopher's job must surely have been the "paperwork." He had to keep an eye on expenses and ensure, as far as he could, that the King was not cheated. It was so easy for—let us say—the master carpenter to arrange for part of a large consignment of timber to be delivered to his own storehouse, to be used for his own purposes, while the King paid the bill. Later, when Sir Christopher was growing old, he was accused of carelessness in allowing this sort of thing to happen, and it may well be that he was a little careless. It is difficult for a man whose head is full of complicated architectural problems, full of the pursuit of beauty and the mysteries of scientific research, to come down to earth sufficiently to be alert to the pilfering of tradesmen. He had a large staff to help him in the office, but the ultimate responsibility was his and his alone.

Lady Wren can have seen little of her brilliant husband. Hardly any details of his family life survive to give us a picture of the home in Scotland Yard. It was just as well perhaps that Faith Coghill, when she married, was no longer a young, romantic girl. Perhaps she was content just to be the wife of such a remarkable man. The short marriage seems to have been a happy one, only marred by the sorrow of little Gilbert's early death. But when Faith herself died, Sir Christopher was not, it seems, inconsolable, for eighteen months later he married again.

This time the bride came from the aristocracy, as was proper, considering Sir Christopher's rise in the world. The new Lady Wren was Jane Fitzwilliam, a sister of Lord Fitzwilliam of Lifford. It all seems to have happened rather suddenly. Perhaps Sir Christopher, having experienced the comfort of a home ruled over by a wife, decided he could not endure to live alone. Perhaps he wanted to give the baby, Christopher, a new mother. Unfortunately, his choice was not good from a practical point of view. Jane was never strong. She gave him two children, a daughter called after herself who was born on November 9, 1677, and a son, William, who arrived two years later and was delicate all his life. This marriage was even shorter than the first. Jane died after a lingering illness (during which Sir Christopher treated her himself by tying a bag of "boglice" around her neck as a cure for the "thrush"!), in October of 1680. Christopher was left with three small children: young Christopher, five; Jane, three; and the baby, William, only a year old. He did not marry again, and the children must have been brought up by nurses. Jane was his favorite. She was musical, and we can imagine her, a grave little girl, being brought down from the nursery to entertain her father on the rare occasions when he spent an evening at home.

During the early 1670's, Sir Christopher had an unusual assignment connected with children, in a macabre way. In 1674 he was supervising the rebuilding of part of the Tower of London when the workmen discovered in a wooden box a pathetic collection of small human bones which were believed to be those of the "Little Princes in the Tower," Edward V and his brother Richard, Duke of York. *Parentalia* gives this description of the event.

> . . . Those two innocent Princes . . . most barbarously murdered there, in their Bed, by their unnatural Uncle, the Usurper, Richard the Third, were, after 191 years found, about 10 Feet deep in the Ground, in a wooden chest, as the Workmen were taking away the stairs, which led from the Royal Lodgings into the Chapel of the white-tower.

The discovery was, of course, told to the King, who asked Sir Christopher to design and have made a suitable container in which the bones could be reburied. *Parentalia* goes on:

> . . . the following warrent from the Lord Chamberlain of His Majestie's Household was directed to the Surveyor, in pursuance whereof, he designed an elegant Urn of white Marble, on a Pedestal, with an inscription; all which being approved by His Majestie, was erected in the East wall of the North-aile of King Henry the Seventh's Chapel.

Were they really the bones of the "Little Princes in the Tower" whose tragic story has been so often told? We shall never know.

II

"Trusty and Well-Beloved"

THE SIX YEARS that passed between Sir Christopher's appointment as Surveyor-General and the laying of St. Paul's foundation stone in 1675 were so full of achievement that it seems almost impossible that one man, even a man of genius, could have accomplished so much. This, too, was the period when, for the first time in his life, he had domestic cares, responsibilities, and sorrows. This is the period of his two marriages, the birth of his four children, the loss of a baby son, and the death of his first wife.

Sir Christopher was a kind man, considerate and patient. He had enemies, as every public man must have—men who envied him his success—but he had more friends than enemies, and his friends loved him deeply. This small man, with gray eyes and a wide mouth that smiled easily, sounds very much like the kind of person who would be devoted to his family. But was he? Could he possibly have done so much work if he had not been single-minded to a fault? Did he go home to dinner every day, talk to his wife, play with his children? If he did, there is no record of it. His close friend and assistant, Robert Hooke, who was often in his home, makes hardly any reference in his diary to Faith or Jane or the children, only recording very briefly that he had been to Lady Wren's funeral, she having died on the previous Monday. Sir John Evelyn records that he stood godfather to one of the Wren boys (William?), but again, he tells us nothing of Sir Christopher's home life.

It is a teasing mystery. Was the kindly man, so valued by his friends, a neglectful husband and father? If he was —and we have no proof of this—the cause must have been, not heartlessness, but his utter devotion to his work. And how he worked! Fifty-one City churches, the Monument, Temple Bar (an ornate gateway), Trinity College Library, the Great Model of St. Paul's, the Royal Observatory, all crowd into these six years.

The Observatory must have been of special interest to Sir Christopher. The Royal Society had been following the work of a young astronomer called Flamsteed; he seemed a very promising fellow. And their interest was justified. When the King's favorite, the Duchess of Portsmouth, introduced to Charles a Frenchman, Sieur de Saint Pierre, who had come to England with an invention to sell, it was Flamsteed who exposed its uselessness. The invention was a means to determine longitude by measuring the moon's distance from certain fixed stars, and had it worked, it would have been an invaluable aid to navigation, as Charles, with his scientific interests, was quick to see. Unfortunately for the Frenchman, Flamsteed was a jump ahead. He was able to demonstrate that, considering the highly uncertain knowledge anyone had of fixed stars, it was impossible to use them for reliable measurement.

Charles turned his attention from Saint Pierre to Flamsteed himself, and appointed him Astronomical Observator. He issued a royal warrant directing the clever young man to "apply himself with the most exact care and dilligence to the rectifying the tables of the motions of the heavens and the places of fixed stars, so as to find out the so-much-desired longitude of phases for the perfecting of the art of navagation." This was highly necessary work. Ships' captains had to steer by the stars, and any information about the stars was of enormous value. It was a time of adventure and exploration. The New World was opening up, new routes were being discovered, and in all the great wastes of sea and sky the sun and stars alone showed the way—if they were interpreted correctly. The new Astronomical Observator was badly needed.

For some years Flamsteed had been working in the round, northeastern turret of the Tower of London, by permission of Sir Jonas Moore, Master of Ordnance. This was the man, a fellow member of the Royal Society, who had gone to inspect the defenses of Tangier in 1663, when Sir Christopher turned down the job. Sir Jonas allowed the Tower armorers to make instruments for Flamsteed, and took a personal interest in his work. So, too, did Sir Christopher, at the time when he was supervising alterations to the White Tower. Sir Christopher, of course, knew Flamsteed and his work through the Royal Society, so he must have been doubly pleased when he was invited by the King to join a committee formed to find a site for an observatory. Flamsteed, through his appointment, was now a court official and could no longer use the Tower of London (that had been a purely private arrangement). New quarters had to be provided for him.

The committee considered various sites in London, but Sir Christopher, always the practical man, urged that an observatory should be set on rising ground. He suggested a site at Greenwich, where the ruins of an old castle could be used as foundations for the new building. Sir Christopher usually had the last word. "Greenwich Hill being mentioned by Sir Christopher Wren, the King approved of it as the most proper"—Flamsteed himself records.

The royal warrant was issued on June 22, 1675, and began:

> Whereas, in order to the finding out of Longitude of Places for perfecting of Navigation and Astronomy. We are resolved to build a small Observatory within Our park at Greenwich, upon the highest ground at or near the Place where the Castle stood with Lodging rooms for Our Observer and Assistant, Our Will and pleasure is that according to such Plot and Design as shall be given you by our trusty and well-beloved Sir Christopher Wren, Knight, . . . you cause the same to be fenced in etc. etc.

To build the observatory, Sir Christopher was given £500, bricks from some demolished fortifications on the banks of the Thames, and a load of unwanted lead from the Tower. With this, and some of the stone from the ruined castle, the work was begun, and by Christmas the roof was on. Thus the world-famous observatory that was in use until recent times came into being. It is a curious building and, architecturally speaking, not representative of Wren's best work, but it was designed for a specific purpose and built with great haste and on a shoestring budget. The King expressed his satisfaction, and Flamsteed was delighted to have a permanent place of work, with living quarters as well.

The Royal Observatory was planned by Sir Christopher in his capacity as Surveyor-General. Another project that he undertook during these busy years was carried out as an act of friendship, and he worked without a fee. Dr. Isaac Barrow had been the Gresham Professor of Geometry and was an old friend. He, like the Wren family, was a Royalist, and some years after the Restoration he gained a reward for his loyalty to the Crown. In 1672 Barrow was appointed to the mastership of Trinity College, Cambridge, and his post at Gresham was filled by one of his pupils, Isaac Newton, the young genius who was later to be president of the Royal Society.

Barrow was a staunch churchman and, like Dr. Sheldon at Oxford, was distressed by the custom of holding the Acts, with their subsequent rowdy behavior, in a church. He longed to build a theater like the Sheldonian, but no one in Cambridge, it seemed, cared enough to support his view by finding the necessary sum of money. Nothing daunted, he decided that, since some money was on hand for the requirements of Trinity College, he would content himself with building a library that would outdo in grandeur any other library in the university. The Trinity Library had been destroyed by fire seven years before, and it was high time that it was rebuilt.

Dr. Barrow set to work to raise more money, writing appeals with his own hand to everyone he could think of, and so persuasive was he that a good sum of money was donated. He chose a site overlooking the river Cam, and asked Sir Christopher to draw up the plans. No doubt he offered the great architect a suitable fee, but Sir Christopher, in the most friendly way, insisted on working for nothing.

As usual, the first plans were greatly modified before building began. The original design was for a circular edifice with a domed roof, but this was changed to a rectangular building with cloisters, the library itself divided into a series of bays. There were various practical considerations to be borne in mind. The site, so near the river, was damp, and books must be preserved from damp. A library building must, above all, be dry, and it must be light. Plenty of windows were necessary, but they must be weatherproof. "By this contrivance," Sir Christopher writes to Dr. Barrow, referring to his design, "the windows of the Library rise high and give place for the deskes against the wall, and being high may be afforded to be large, and being wide may have stone mullions and the glass pointed, which after all inventions is the only durable way in our Climate for a publique building where care must be taken that the snowe drive not in."

When the building was finished, the outside was, in the opinion of some people, a little dull. But no one had anything but praise for the interior, where Sir Christopher's practical mind had produced working conditions that have never been bettered. The great room was divided into bays by bookshelves standing at right angles to the walls, so that each student could work in a "celle," as they were then called, of his own. Sir Christopher writes:

> The disposition of the Shelves both along the walls and breaking out from the walls must needes prove very convenient and gracefull, and the best way for the students will be to have a little square table in each Celle with two chairs.

Generations of Trinity College students have worked at the little square tables in the cells. Over and over again, we find that the Wren planning was so enlightened, so practical and well thought out, that it is impossible to improve on it to any great extent.

Considerably later, Grinling Gibbons, the young man who had been discovered by Sir John Evelyn and who was now very much in demand for his delicate carvings, adorned the new library with wreaths of flowers and the royal cipher. The ceiling had to be left plain, for the money ran out—as money has a habit of doing. The plans Sir Christopher had drawn up for the decoration of the ceiling were not carried out for another two centuries.

Sir Christopher had hardly finished his work in Cambridge when he was asked to design another library, this time by Dean Honywood of Lincoln. Honywood was a

Royalist who had left England during Cromwell's time and gone to Utrecht in Holland, where he had built up a large collection of valuable books. At the Restoration he came home and was appointed to the deanery at Lincoln Cathedral. The cathedral had suffered at the hands of Cromwell's troops, and there was a great deal to do before things were back to normal. A library to house all the books the Dean had amassed during his exile had to wait. But at last, in 1674, the time came, and again Sir Christopher Wren was asked to undertake the work. Once more, careful planning allied to the Wren genius for creating beautiful buildings produced a library that delighted Honywood, who then donated his collection of books to the cathedral.

Meanwhile, work on the City churches was going steadily forward. Twenty-six of the fifty-one were nearly completed. Their names read like a poem: St. Mary-le-Bow, St. Bride's, St. Lawrence Jewry, St. Magnus the Martyr, St. Benet Fink, St. Stephen's Walbrook, and many more. Among these churches, it is generally considered, may be found the best work Sir Christopher had done up to that time.

Wren's work may have been exacting, but no one could say it was monotonous. The great variety of buildings he was called upon to design, both privately and in his official capacity, was amazing: chapels, libraries, parish churches, palaces, monuments, and, presently, homes for old and disabled soldiers and sailors, came from his drawing board in a continuous stream. A good many private houses are today described as Wren buildings, but it is doubtful if he had much to do with them. Domestic architecture was not really his line, but probably, in order to be obliging, he threw out an idea, leaving it to his assistants to draw up the plans.

Temple Bar, however, is believed to be his work, undertaken in his official capacity as a servant of the Crown. It was a difficult assignment. He had to build a dramatic and dignified archway across the narrow thoroughfare of Fleet Street, to mark the spot where, by tradition, the Lord Mayor of London meets the Sovereign whenever it is his or her pleasure to visit the City. The arch is now gone, removed to the country, as traffic worsened and Fleet Street had to be widened. But the tradition remains.

The arch was built of Portland stone, a very white stone quarried on the Isle of Portland, in the county of Dorset—a queer, wild area of land joined to the mainland by a narrow causeway. A large part of the new City was built of this stone, including St. Paul's and many other public buildings. The stone was brought from the so-called island by sea. When new, it was dazzlingly white, but the soot-laden air of London soon turned it a uniform gray. The archway, when completed, was very grand. Above the middle arch was a guardroom; on either side were huge pillars and niches containing statues. Right at the top were iron spikes upon which the severed heads of traitors could be, and frequently were, displayed. And what the civilized and humane Sir Christopher felt about this, we can only guess. It was the accepted custom of those strange times, when culture and barbarism still existed side by side.

With all this official work in London, and his private commitments in the university towns and elsewhere, Sir Christopher might have been excused, one would think, from undertaking any other work overseas. But no, he was the King's Surveyor-General, and when a hospital for disabled soldiers was required in Ireland, it was his duty to design it.

The French had recently built Les Invalides, a home for old, sick army pensioners, and Charles was not going to be outdone in humanity by the French. Friends the two nations might—precariously—be, but there was still rivalry between them. The hospital in Dublin was not actually built until some years later, but the idea was first put forward in 1675. It was one more thing to occupy the Surveyor-General's mind.

Now an eventful day was drawing near, the day Sir Christopher had been working toward ever since the Great Fire nine years before. Wearisome discussion must end sometime, and architect Wren, sick and tired of delay, decided the day had come. "From that time the Surveyor resolved to make no more models or publickly expose his Drawings," says a contemporary report. The final design for St. Paul's, the "Warrent design," was at last approved by the King, and by the end of 1675 the building of the new cathedral was begun.

Part IV

A TIME OF ACHIEVEMENT

. . . we must earnestly desire your presence and assistance with all speed.

LETTER FROM THE DEAN OF ST. PAUL'S

12

St. Paul's Begun

LET US TRAVEL BACK IN TIME to the summer of 1675. In the office of the King's Surveyor-General the fire that had burned all winter on the hearth was allowed to die out as warm sunshine streamed through the windows and lit up the mass of papers lying on Sir Christopher Wren's desk. Outside, in the pleasant gardens of Whitehall, trees were in young leaf, lilac bloomed, and the courtiers, fine as peacocks in their silks and velvets, strolled under the mild skies and planned water picnics for the days ahead. Housewives all over London began their great spring cleaning.

But the housewives in the vicinity of St. Paul's were in despair. Demolition had begun in earnest, and dust penetrated even tightly closed windows and lay in a thick film over furniture newly polished with beeswax, over carpets and hangings. It got into the very food; you could feel the grit between your teeth as you bit into your bread or beef. And the noise! It gave the housewife a headache, made the dogs bark and the babies cry. The workmen were using battering rams, as if it were the olden days and St. Paul's a castle under siege. And as if this was not bad enough, a soldier from the Tower had been sent for to blow up part of the old ruin with gunpowder. No one was surprised when a large chunk of stone flew out and crashed into the balcony of a nearby house. It was only to be expected, when such dangerous methods were used. What was Sir Christopher Wren about, to allow these things to happen? How long would this nuisance endure?

There was to be no peace for the neighborhood housewives for a long time to come. The demolition was slow. It went on, in stages, for years, and the noise of destruction was rivaled by the noise of construction as wagons laden with brick, stone, and timber rumbled over the cobbled streets. The air was filled with the ring of hammer on chisel, the creaking of machinery as great blocks of stone were hoisted into place, the shouts of men, and the clatter of horses' hoofs. No peace for the householder or the shopkeeper, but triumph in the heart of Sir Christopher Wren, as the great work of his life at last began.

It was ten years since St. Paul's Cathedral had first become a part of Sir Christopher's life, ten years since he first submitted plans to renovate the old building, before the Great Fire. It was nine years since he had constructed the first model, two years since the Great Model had met with a qualified acceptance. All the time he had been working on other projects—the City churches, libraries, monuments, and the Royal Observatory—the plans for St. Paul's had been on his drawing board, constantly revised, always in his thoughts. And now at last the royal warrant was granted and the work had begun. Private cares and sorrows were pushed aside as Sir Christopher, his slight, frail body gratefully drawing warmth from the May sunshine, stood in St. Paul's Churchyard, watching dreams being translated into the reality of stone.

He had been through many trials and tribulations before the final design met with acceptance, and he was certainly desperately disappointed when the Great Model was rejected, possibly on the grounds that it bore a resemblance to St. Peter's in Rome and was on that account suspected of Popery. The "Warrent design" was not, in Sir Christopher's opinion, nearly as good, but he managed, shrewdly, to obtain permission to make such changes as he found necessary as the building went on.

The foundation stone was laid on June 21, 1675, with no ceremony at all. No one knows who laid the stone, whether Sir Christopher himself, Mr. Strong, the foreman of works, or someone else. It seems strange that such an important occasion should not have been made a public affair attended by the King and church dignitaries, but it was not. In any case, the laying of the stone was not immediately followed by the raising up of new walls but by months of excavation and demolition. The new cathedral, when completed, would be tremendously heavy, and it was necessary to do a thorough study of what there might be underground, before starting to rebuild. It was as well that this was done. At some time, on the northeast corner of the site, a deep pit had been dug going right down through the apparently firm top layer to shifting sand below. There was nothing to be done but dig down through the sand until solid earth was reached, a depth of forty feet. Then a stone pier ten feet square had to be built to support what would be the northeast corner of the chancel.

The old St. Paul's had been sturdily built. The walls, although judged unsafe, were still so solid that the battering rams—huge "masts" of timber ending in an iron spike—had little effect until gunpowder was used to undermine the foundations. The delay gave Sir Christopher time to go back to the drawing board and, taking full advantage of the wording of the royal warrant, to put right many things he had felt to be wrong in the "Warrent design."

Since, above all, a huge public building must be safe, the dome, upon which Christopher's heart was set, presented grave problems. The space under the dome, inside, had to be very large, as this was the main part of the cathedral, with the nave, aisles, transepts, and chancel all branching from it. Outside, the dome must be built to a great height—and it was done not with brick, like the inner dome, but with timber covered with lead. On top of this was to be a stone lantern or steeple surmounted by a ball and cross.

The construction of this enormous dome was a fascinating mathematical exercise, the most complex that Sir Christopher had ever faced. Nor was it a question of pure mathematics, for practical considerations always had to be kept in mind. It was useless to design a portico of huge stone columns when the Portland quarries could not produce blocks of stone suitable for columns more than four feet in diameter. Sir Christopher went down to Portland himself—a weary journey, over bad roads—to learn at first hand just exactly what the masons there could or could not produce. A disastrous landslip that completely wiped out the King's quarry added to the difficulty of getting exactly the stone needed, and would have held up the building if arrangements had not been made immediately with the other quarries, which were privately owned. With all the rebuilding going on in London, every stone quarry in the land was working to capacity. Sir Christopher had to use his authority as Surveyor-General to get priority for St. Paul's.

An odd incident occurred one day when Sir Christopher was on the cathedral site. We can picture him standing with the stonemasons among the rubble of the demolished walls. In the distance the repeated blows of the battering ram echo through the ruins of the old building, almost drowning the everyday sounds of a great city, now so triumphantly springing back to life. A fine dust from the powdered stone dims the color of Sir Christopher's clothes and settles on his full-bottomed wig. He talks earnestly to the foreman mason and then, turning to one of the workmen, he says: "Bring me a piece of stone from that pile over there. Anything will do, so that it will act as a marker."

The man goes over to the pile and picks up the first stone that comes to hand. He lays it in the spot Sir Christopher indicates, and then everyone present stares at it in silence, struck by the curious chance that has brought this stone and no other to be laid as a marker in what will be the heart of the cathedral. For the stone so casually selected is part of an old gravestone, and carved into it, still clearly discernible, is the word RESURGAM: I shall rise again.

It was at about this time that an event occurred which had all London laughing. Sir Robert Viner, the Lord Mayor, decided that it would be a tactful gesture to put up a statue to the King, who was doing so much to help and encourage the citizens to rebuild their city. No need, thought the Mayor, to consult Sir Christopher Wren. This had nothing to do with the Surveyor of Works. Sir Christopher had such expensive ideas and he, Sir Robert, knew of a way to provide a statue at a very reasonable cost.

The Polish ambassador in England had recently ordered from Poland a statue of the King of Poland, with the idea of erecting it somewhere in London to commemorate a victory of the Poles over the Turks. For some reason, however, he had never carried out his project and the statue was still in its packing case at Tower Dock, unclaimed, the shipping dues unpaid. Sir Robert Viner discovered it could be purchased very cheaply; he went down to Tower Dock.

The statue, when unpacked, was found to be the Polish king astride his horse, a vanquished Turk prone under the charger's hoofs. Sir Robert was delighted. A different head on the horseman, and it would be Charles II to the life! The prostrate Turk could represent Oliver Cromwell, after a few necessary changes had been made. He bought the statue and commissioned a sculptor to carve a new head for Charles and attend to the Turk. Rather a botched-up affair, one may think, and yet all might have been well if the sculptor had done his job properly. Unfortunately, he forgot to remove the Turk's headdress. When the statue was unveiled, there lay Oliver Cromwell —in a turban! The whole penny-pinching plot was revealed, and London laughed at her mayor. For fifty years the statue remained one of the City's great jokes, until someone in authority had the good sense to have it removed.

IN 1680 SIR CHRISTOPHER lost his second wife, Jane, and his few years of married domesticity were over. The five-year-old Christopher and his little half sister and brother had all the comforts and advantages their father's position could give them, but it must have been a deprived childhood for them, left to the care of servants. Perhaps Sir Christopher's sisters took pity on them and had them stay in their country homes. Susan, who had been a second mother to Sir Christopher, might well have had a hand in the upbringing of his motherless children. Of their father they probably did not see very much. He was so busy, so much in demand. He and Robert Hooke, now his devoted assistant, spent much of their leisure time in coffeehouses, those forerunners of clubs, which were becoming popular all over London. They were good places in which to relax, and different groups of people soon adopted their own coffeehouses. If you wanted to meet writers, you went to Garraways or Child's; businessmen could be found at Lloyds, a name that has lived on and is known worldwide. The proprietors of these establishments provided the daily and weekly newspapers, and sold not only tea and coffee but the new popular drink, chocolate. Sir Christopher and Robert Hooke favored Garraways in Cornhill, Child's in St. Paul's Churchyard, and Man's, of Chancery Lane, all in the City of London and conveniently close to their work. There they sat, toasting themselves in front of a bright, sea-coal fire, sipping their hot chocolate and talking of everything under the sun.

In his diary for February 1678, Hooke writes:

> With Sir Christopher at coffee-house. Spoke of his Theory of Respiration, Muscular Motion etc. delivered to Mr Boyle. Shewed me his draught of Mausoleum (for Charles I at Windsor.)

And on another occasion he noted:

> With Aubrey [the diarist] to Sir Chr. Wren at Palsgrave Head. Sir Chr. Wren's birthday. He paid all . . . Good discourse.

The very next day Hooke, full of affection for Sir Christopher, who was always such good company and who "paid all," sent a hobbyhorse to young Christopher which cost him every penny of fourteen shillings, a large sum to spend on a toy.

They talked and talked, these clever, alert men, in many ways ahead of their times. "Discourced about petrification of Bodys, about plaister, about forming of glasse, form of arches, light gold statues, staining marble . . . about printing stuffs and guilding stuffs . . . about ghosts and spirits."

Perhaps Sir Christopher told the story of his adventure when staying with a Mr. Mompesson at Tydworth. He saw nothing out of the ordinary, but he heard a drumming, "as one may drum with one's hand upon wainscot." He noticed that this drumming only occurred when a certain maidservant was in the next room, and also that the knocking seldom came after twelve o'clock at night or before six in the morning. This seems to have thrown suspicion on the maidservant, but this particular haunting was very persistent, and at the time it was, apparently, accepted as a genuine ghost.

Sir Christopher could have told another strange tale, the tale of the dream he had when he lay ill in Paris. The doctor wanted to bleed him, as was the custom then for almost everything, but Sir Christopher was reluctant to agree. Even though he was in great pain, he put it off until the next day. His son tells the story in *Parentalia:*

> That night he dreamt that he was in a place where Palm-trees grew (suppose Egypt) and that a Woman in a romantick Habit reached him Dates. The next day he sent for Dates, which cured him of the Pain.

This was a fortunate and timely dream. It must have been much more pleasant to eat dates than to submit to being bled, but a medical explanation of this unlikely cure would be most interesting.

SIR CHRISTOPHER had need of all the relaxation he could get, for the work piled up, and he was constantly on the move. All the King's residences were under his care, and much had to be done to keep them in good order. There were trips to Windsor, some miles from London, to oversee work on the castle there; private trips to Cambridge to see the new library through its final stages; and always there was St. Paul's, needing constant supervision.

Early in the 1680's he began a new work only second in importance to the cathedral. The building, which took ten years to complete, was a hospital and home for old soldiers, a far more ambitious affair than the one built in Dublin a few years earlier. This was a project very much after the King's heart, but most of the money for it was to come not from the impoverished King but from an old friend of Sir Christopher's, Sir Stephen Fox, Paymaster-General of the Army. Fox had been with the King during his exile, and at the restoration he was rewarded for his loyalty by being appointed to a lucrative post in the army. His money affairs prospered, and by 1682 he had put by a very comfortable fortune, "honestly got and unenvied which is almost a miracle," notes Evelyn in his diary, for he too was a friend of Sir Stephen Fox.

It may have been Sir Christopher's account of the hospital he had built for old soldiers in Ireland which first put the idea into Sir Stephen's head. Or it may have been the

Courtesy The Guildhall Library, London

The Royal Observatory in Greenwich Park

The New York Public Library Picture Collection

A contemporary drawing of Wren's Temple Bar, from *The Illustrated London News*

Courtesy The Guildhall Library, London

St. Mary-le-Bow Church, designed by Sir Christopher Wren

Courtesy The Guildhall Library, London

Exterior of St. Stephen's Church, Walbrook

Courtesy The Guildhall Library, London

Interior of St. Stephen's Church, Walbrook

Courtesy The Guildhall Library, London

The demolition of old St. Paul's after the great fire, from a contemporary drawing by Wych

Courtesy The Guildhall Library, London

A contemporary view of The Royal Hospital at Chelsea

Courtesy The Guildhall Library, London

An artist's rendering of a Chelsea pensioner

example of the French, who had built Les Invalides. At any rate, once the idea came to him, he determined to devote a large part of his fortune to such a hospital, and of course his old friend Sir Christopher Wren was the only man who could plan it for him.

Next came the hunt for a site, and this was finally settled in a most satisfactory way. Just after the Great Fire, when the Royal Society had been homeless, Charles II had presented them with a plot of land in the village of Chelsea, a few miles from the City, on the banks of the Thames. It was a charming spot, but quite impractical for the Royal Society, being too far out of town for the members to meet there easily. The present, in fact, was a white elephant and an embarrassment to the Society. It is necessary to be tactful over presents from a King, however. They had hoped to get rid of it when the Observatory was built—it was one of the sites suggested—but Sir Christopher had been obliged to go against the interests of the Society there, realizing as he did that an Observatory should be on rising ground.

It was a tricky situation, and for fourteen years the Chelsea fields lay empty of anything but cows and sheep. Now, however, came the perfect solution. The King would buy back the site from the Royal Society, paying very little for it, since it had been a gift in the first place, and he would then present it to the army for the hospital that the Paymaster-General proposed to build. This arrangement satisfied everyone. The Society was at last rid of an unwanted gift, the King was able to make a splendid gesture at very small expense, and Sir Stephen could begin to build his hospital.

The three friends—Wren, Evelyn, and Fox—discussed the whole scheme thoroughly, sitting over Sir Stephen's study fire. Sir Christopher was, of course, to be the architect, but Sir John Evelyn had ideas of his own. The plans, he insisted, "must embrace a library," and he "mentioned several books since some soldiers might possibly be studious." The hospital was to house four hundred old men, and this meant employing quite a large staff. "We arranged the governor, chaplaine, steward, housekeeper, surgeon, cook, butler, gardener, porter and other officers, with their several salaries and entertainments," notes Evelyn in his diary.

Sir Christopher planned the buildings around a large central court, facing south, with the accommodation making three sides of the square. The central range, approached by a most impressive portico, consisted of a dining hall and a chapel. The two wings, each three stories high, with attics above, were the living and sleeping quarters for the pensioners. The hospital was built of brick with stone coigns and ornamental woodwork painted white. It was, and still is, beautiful and practical. Sir Christopher never lost sight of its function, the comfortable housing of old and sick men. The staircase has shallow treads, to make the way up and down safe for old feet, and a wide rail to which old hands may cling. The wards are light and airy. The sun shines full on the dining hall where the pensioners meet for meals. Grinling Gibbons carved a magnificent statue of Charles II in Roman dress, and this, cast in bronze, was set in the courtyard to commemorate his part in this most humane work. The fortunate old soldiers moved in, and for three hundred years the Chelsea pensioner in his distinctive red coat has been a familiar part of the London scene.

13

The Palace That Never Was

> King Charles II, taking a Liking to the Situation of Winchester, by reason of the deliciousness of the Country for all manner of Country Sports, set Sir Christopher Wren, that great Architect . . . to make a plan for a Royal Palace where the Old Castle stood . . . It will be the finest Palace in England when finished and inferior to few abroad.

IT WAS AN AMBITIOUS PROJECT, this palace of Winchester. In the same year that Chelsea Hospital was begun, Charles gave Sir Christopher a free hand to build him a glorified hunting seat in the old town that is the capital of the county of Hampshire in the south of England. The King had recently lost by fire his home at Newmarket, where he had laid out a racecourse and encouraged the training of horses. It was a great blow, and perhaps partly on this account he turned his attention to the other side of England, to Winchester. He already spent much of his time there. It was a famous place for hunting and hawking. The New Forest with its deer was not far away, and there was splendid hare coursing on the smooth turf of the Downs. Here the King sought relaxation from the cares of state, from his difficult, quarrelsome subjects, from religious controversy, money troubles, and the whole, wretched business of the Monmouth Rebellion. The Duke of Monmouth was his natural son, a handsome, upstanding boy whom Charles would have been only too glad to acknowledge as his heir. The boy was the son of Lucy Walter, whom Charles had met when he was only eighteen, during his exile in Holland. Charles had been very fond of James Croft, as the boy was known, received him at court, made him Duke of Monmouth. And how had James rewarded him? Made nothing but trouble, marching and fighting and stirring up ill feeling with his absurd allegations that he, and not James, the King's brother, was the rightful heir to the throne.

But here, on the windy uplands within sight, from an eminence, of the fleet riding at anchor at Spithead, the King hoped to find peace. Sir Christopher should build for him no mere shooting lodge but a palace standing in a park eight miles around and with a wide street leading directly to Winchester Cathedral, a street lined with splendid houses for the members of the court. And that good fellow, Wren, must make haste and get it all done as quickly as possible, for the King was growing old—not perhaps in years, for he was only fifty-five, but in spirit. He had lived every moment of his life to the utmost. He was known as the Merry Monarch and certainly, since coming into his kingdom, he had squeezed all the enjoyment out of life that he could. But there had been strain as well as fun, hard work as well as sport, poverty as well as riches. He had faced death, and seen those he loved die. He had been forced to watch his adored sister, Minette, made wretched by a disastrous marriage until her mysterious and disquieting death.

Sometimes, in moments of depression, the King wondered if he would ever live to see his fine new residence completed. Sir Christopher must make haste. Let him employ more men, and push the work on.

Sir Christopher divided his time between Chelsea—where the hospital was rising slowly from the green meadows by the Thames—the City and St. Paul's, and the windy heights above Winchester. He was constantly on the road. Did he amuse himself, during these tedious journeys, with his way-wiser, fastened beneath the coach and seen through a little window cut in the floor? There is one thing we can be sure of: his brain was never idle, and with his wide interests, he can never have been bored.

The palace at Winchester rose at an astounding rate. In shape it was similar to Chelsea Hospital, being built around three sides of a courtyard, with great marble pillars flanking the main entrance in the central block. There were two chapels: one for the King, a Protestant; and one for the Queen, a Catholic. There were sixteen huge rooms in each wing, and a noble staircase leading to the guardroom on the first floor. Three cupolas were planned, one for each wing, the central cupola to be set so high that from it the King could see his men-of-war lying off Portsmouth, miles away. The Duke of Tuscany had sent marble pillars to support the portico of the great staircase. They would look very fine when they were unpacked and set in place at last. Sir Christopher, as the third year of building dawned, urged the workmen on.

But it was too late. On a cold February day in the year 1685, Charles II died as bravely as he had lived, and his ineffectual brother, James, became the new king.

Down in Hampshire, the bitter winter winds blew through the uncompleted palace, moaning along the empty corridors, whistling through the unglazed windows, as rain dripped desolately from the newly finished roof. The army of workmen were "stood off" until the wishes of the new king were known.

It was an anxious time for Sir Christopher. He owed his appointment as Surveyor-General to the personal friendship of King Charles. Although he must have felt reasonably secure, being now acknowledged the leading architect in the country, still, one never knew. And even if his post was safe, what of Winchester Palace? Would King James wish to go on with that?

King James did not wish it. He was not such a dedicated sportsman as his elder brother had been. He saw no need to have still another expensive residence to keep up, and in the wilds of Hampshire too. No more money should be spent on this glorified hunting lodge. For himself, he wished the Surveyor-General to turn his attention to the palace of Whitehall, for which he had great plans.

The empty shell of Charles II's costly toy at Winchester stood silent and abandoned—the palace that never was.

Now began drastic changes in Whitehall to please the new king. James's first wife, Anne Hyde, had died, leaving him with two daughters, Mary and Anne, both in their time to rule England. He had married again, an Italian princess, Mary of Modena, a Catholic like himself, and it was partly to please her that the alterations were made. He commanded Sir Christopher to build a range of large buildings running from the existing banqueting hall nearly to the Thames. There was to be a long gallery, a grand staircase, new apartments for the Queen, a new chapel, and a council chamber. These buildings, like Chelsea Hospital, were built in brick with stone dressings, a style very popular at the time, and of lasting beauty. The interior was sumptuous to a degree, with marble chimney pieces and pillars, painted ceilings, and a wonderful wrought-iron balustrade, the first of its kind Sir Christopher had had the chance to commission. A further extension of the Queen's apartments was planned, with formal gardens on the Embankment to take the place of a stretch of unsavory tidal mud. But before this could be done, James's short reign came to an end. England did not want him any longer, and he fled to France, where his wife had already gone, together with her baby son, about whom there had been much mystery and controversy. This was the child (later to be known as the Old Pretender) believed by many to have been smuggled into Queen Mary's bed in a warming pan, her own child having died at birth. It seems an unlikely story, in view of the fact that Mary's bedroom was packed with important people at the time of the birth. This was the custom and was designed to prevent just such a substitution as a certain faction now claimed had taken place. However, true or false, people had had enough of the bungling James and his Catholic wife. They preferred his Protestant daughter Mary, and her sober, responsible young husband, William of Orange from the Netherlands. They invited Mary to be their queen, with William as her consort.

But this did not suit William. He was not prepared to be Mary's consort, he said. He and his wife must come to England on equal terms, or he would not come at all. After anxious consultation, it was agreed that this was the best plan. Perhaps the English felt that two heads were better than one. So William and Mary it was—and the young couple were given a tremendous reception with all the usual bonfires, church bells, and gun salutes. People noted that Mary did not seem in the least upset at taking her father's place. She was in high spirits and got up early on her first morning as Queen to roam around Whitehall. "She ran about, looking into every closet and conveniency, and turned up the quilts of the beds, just as people do at an inn, with no sort of concern in her appearance," the Duchess of Marlborough noted disapprovingly. This casual attitude upset some people who thought she should have shown more concern about the banishment of her father. But everyone, except the Catholics, approved of her husband, who gave the impression of being a serious, thoughtful young man, though inclined to be cold and withdrawn.

Sir Christopher did not allow himself to be drawn into controversial matters. He was a servant of the Crown, and whoever was the reigning monarch of the time, he was there to carry out his wishes. And how many changes there were during his long life! Born during the reign of Charles I, he lived through the years of the Commonwealth, through the reigns of Charles II, James II, William and Mary, Anne, and finally, George I. Patiently, he tried to satisfy all their whims. It must have been heartbreaking to leave Winchester Palace half finished—and now the same thing was happening at Whitehall.

William did not care for Whitehall. It lay too low and was unhealthy, he considered. It was bad for his asthma. He explored, and found Hampton Court, a beautiful Tudor building on the banks of the Thames some miles upriver from London. The situation was perfect, but the building, he decided, was old-fashioned and fit only to be pulled down. The Surveyor-General must build something more suitable for a royal residence in this charming spot.

Sir Christopher remembered the greatest of all the French châteaux—Versailles—which he had studied during his stay in France. If his first plans had been adopted, there might have arisen an English Versailles on the banks of the Thames. But again he was disappointed. Plans were changed and the demolition was halted. In the end, part of the ambitious new design was welded onto the old Tudor building. British compromise had triumphed again.

Sir Christopher's patience and even temper must often have been sorely tried in his dealings with royalty. One can imagine him, as he drew up the first set of plans, smiling wryly in anticipation of the alterations he would have to make before the building actually arose—if it ever did. Of his more important works, only two were completely carried out to his satisfaction: Chelsea Hospital and St. Paul's Cathedral.

What comfort he must have taken from St. Paul's. There at least the work went on steadily, there his word and his wishes carried weight with the multitude of people concerned in the rebuilding. When he was worn out with the whimsies of kings and queens, he could always find consolation in St. Paul's. He had a new assistant now, a brilliant young man called Nicholas Hawksmoor, whom he employed as "scholar and domestic clerk." Nicholas joined him in 1679 at the age of eighteen, and Sir Christopher found him a very useful member of his team. The team consisted of the Assistant Surveyor, John Oliver; Hawksmoor; the ever faithful Robert Hooke; and the master masons, Thomas and Edward Strong. There were others, but these were the men upon whom Christopher knew he could always rely.

At St. Paul's, then, all was sanity. It was soothing, after a morning of dealing with the vagaries of the Queen or with William's obstinate determination to have his own way, to walk around the great building with the men who were nearest to him. He liked to talk to Grinling Gibbons about his fine carvings in wood; to Cibber, working on a huge stone Phoenix to be placed above the southern portico; to Jean Tijou, an inspired Frenchman whose wrought-iron work has never been equaled; or to Sir James Thornhill, the artist commissioned to decorate the interior of the dome. Sir Christopher was not quite happy about these paintings, they were not entirely to his taste—but he loved the work of the other men.

King William was having difficulty raising enough public money to complete the alterations at Hampton Court. Parliament, which had to vote the money, did not like the idea of the reigning monarchs living so far outside London. Ministers of state, traveling down to see them, might well be set upon by highwaymen. It was a long coach ride from the center of London, and the road led over desolate stretches of country, very dangerous even in broad daylight. If Whitehall was, as William insisted, bad for his asthma, then other accommodation must be found. Unwillingly, William proposed to purchase Nottingham House in Kensington, and unwillingly Parliament finally agreed. Kensington was a village considerably nearer to the center of things than Hampton Court, but even so, it was a bit out of the way and the risk of highwaymen, although diminished, was still there. Moreover, Nottingham House was quite unsuited for a royal residence. It would take large sums of money to bring it up to the standard required.

William dug in his toes. His health was of the first importance. He would not spend his time gasping and wheezing in the damp rabbit warrens of Whitehall. If he was not to be allowed to live permanently in the pure air of Hampton, then his town residence must be Kensington. Parliament gave in, and Sir Christopher Wren was instructed to turn Nottingham House into Kensington Palace.

Funds, however, were still inadequate, and Sir Christopher had to compromise. The new palace could be grand outside or convenient within. The State Apartments were considered more important than anything else, since it was here that foreign dignitaries would be received, and so the exterior of the building was not altered as much as the King and Queen and their architect would have wished. Sir John Evelyn went to see the finished work of his old friend, and wrote in his diary: "I went to Kensington, which King William bought of Lord Nottingham and altered, but was yet a patched building, but with the garden, however, it is a very sweete villa, having to it the Park and a straight new way through this Park." Some years later Sir Christopher added a Banqueting Hall or Orangery, as it was called, an expensive and beautiful addition, but even then Evelyn was not enthusiastic about the place. "Noble, but not great," he notes, rather grudgingly. But William and Mary were satisfied. Compared with Whitehall, Kensington was positively cozy. The large windows of the King's Gallery caught the sun, and the Queen's Gallery with its two fireplaces and deep window seats was a pleasant place for Mary to sit with her ladies on cold winter days. Once again the gifted, patient Surveyor-General had managed to satisfy his royal masters and yet imprint on the building the marks of his own good taste. "Sir Christopher Wren could not build a common brick house without imposing his character on it" was the comment of a writer at the time.

Sir Christopher's children were now out of early childhood and able to be more companionable with their father. Young Christopher was fourteen when William and Mary came to the throne, and was at Eton College, the school for the sons of gentlemen which stands almost under the shadow of Windsor Castle. Jane was twelve and already showing an aptitude for music. Her father had her taught to play the organ and took pride in her ability. William was still delicate, too delicate to send away to school. He must have been very dependent on his sister Jane for company in the big house in Scotland Yard.

How did they spend their days, these motherless children of a busy, preoccupied father? There would have been visiting tutors to teach William Greek and Latin and, most likely, mathematics and other scientific subjects. Jane, perhaps, studied with him. She must have been a bright little girl or her father would never have made a companion of her, as we know he did. But did he ever find time to take them on excursions? Did he take them to the wonderful fair on the frozen Thames, when the ice was so thick that stalls were set up, fires lit, and oxen roasted whole? He and Robert Hooke once visited Bartholomew Fair, where they saw an elephant "wave colours, shoot a gun, bend and kneel, carry a castle and a man," which would have amused William and Jane—but did he take them to see the wonderful elephant? Nobody tells us if he did. It was splendid, of course, to have a father who was intimate with kings and queens and all the important men of the day, to live in a big house and have a coach and a footman, but it might have been more fun to be the children of a country parson in a place like East Knoyle, to run wild in simple, comfortable clothes, to have ponies and dogs, to go primrosing in the spring and nutting in the fall, to gather holly and ivy from the woods at Christmas and decorate the house for the carol singers and mummers who were sure to come around on Christmas Eve.

It must have been a great day for Jane and William when half-brother Christopher came home for the holidays, to form a link between the schoolroom and the exciting but awe-inspiring world in which their famous father played so large a part. For the eighties were busy years for Sir Christopher, quite apart from his architectural work. For two years he was president of the Royal Society, and all through the decade he continued to sit on committees to investigate new scientific work. He, Robert Hooke, and his old friend Seth Ward were always seeking a really satisfactory method of finding longitude at sea, a pressing need for the navigators who were boldly forging new links with far-off countries. Wealth poured into London from strange lands all over the globe, but too many ships set sail and were never heard of again, blown off-course and lost. Sir Christopher turned his attention from palaces, banqueting halls, grand staircases, and porticoes to consult long and earnestly with his friends, to work out mathematical problems, seeking to find a "safe conduct" for mariners lost in the huge, tractless oceans of the world.

In 1684 the architect Hugh May died, and his work on Windsor Castle was taken over by Sir Christopher. Fortunately, it was all but finished, so he was able to find time to join the council of the Hudson Bay Company and to do a little private speculation in land. London was still rebuilding, and not only rebuilding but expanding. There was money to be made if land in the city could be bought reasonably and resold. The salary of the Surveyor-General was not enormous; more money was really needed to keep up a good household and send young Christopher to Oxford when he left Eton. Sir Christopher went into partnership with a man called Roger Jackson, ventured a large sum of money on land speculation, and made a handsome profit. In 1685 he stood for Parliament and was a Member for two years, long enough to bring in a bill for the finishing of Chelsea Hospital. The money was raised by putting a tax on hackney coaches, the forerunner of the motor tax of modern times.

As the decade came to an end, Sir Christopher, now nearly sixty, was as busy as he had ever been in his life.

14

Gathering Clouds

IN THE LIVES OF MOST PEOPLE, there comes a time when things do not run smoothly. Up until the last years of the century, Sir Christopher seems to have had remarkably good fortune, apart from private griefs. He slipped into a high position to which he was not, perhaps, really entitled; he enjoyed the favor of kings; and very few voices were raised in criticism of his work. He had every reason to be contented, for he had work that he loved, varied interests to occupy his leisure, fairly good health, staunch friends, and enough money to meet all his needs. His calm temperament cushioned him against the small difficulties of everyday life. On October 20, 1692, his sixtieth birthday, Sir Christopher Wren must have felt that all was set fair for a tranquil old age.

But before the seventeenth century died, his troubles began; and they came through the Comptroller of Works, William Talman, a man with whom even the equable Sir Christopher found it hard to agree.

William Talman was himself an architect and a good one, so when, in his official capacity, he reported that much of the new masonry at Hampton Court was unsound, his report could not be ignored. Sir Christopher was summoned to face the charge before the Lords of the Treasury.

Now it must be remembered that Sir Christopher was always being urged to make haste. James II had wanted Whitehall renovated in the shortest possible time; William and Mary wanted Hampton Court remodeled quickly; and when a house was needed in a more convenient position, then Kensington Palace must arise as if by magic. In these circumstances, Sir Christopher decided to take a calculated risk. He had some of the outer walls of both palaces built in brick "while forming the interior with crossed timber partitions on which he balanced the chimney breasts and heavy brick stacks." He had used his method successfully at Whitehall, but at Hampton Court and Kensington Palace it led to disaster. Walls collapsed, and workmen were killed. How much Sir Christopher's method was to blame for this, it is difficult to say. The construction may have been successful at Whitehall because he himself had been able to keep an eye on the work as it progressed. Both at Hampton Court and Kensington he had had to leave far more responsibility to the contractors because of the difficulties of traveling into the country, and it may well be that the contractors scamped the work. But it was Sir Christopher who had to meet the charge.

Talman asserted that the great blocks of masonry between the windows of the south front at Hampton Court were cracked, "so that a man might put his fingers in." A witness for Sir Christopher indignantly denied this, saying that only four were cracked and then by a hairsbreadth. Talman contended that the cracks had been filled with plaster and that, moreover, the pillars had been "crampt with iron to keep them together." Wren retorted: "What was done for greater caution ought not to be maliciously interpreted."

In the end the Lords of the Treasury did the only possible thing. They appointed "indifferent persons to view the same and see if the building will stand or no." The report of the "indifferent persons"—that is, people who had no part in the affair—was in Sir Christopher's favor, and the building continued, with an uneasy truce between architect and Comptroller of Works. Years later Talman's dislike, or possibly jealousy, of Sir Christopher bubbled up again. He accused him of being unkind to a nephew of his. Sir Christopher, he said, had promised to help the young man and then gone back on his word. The letter Sir Christopher wrote, fully justifying himself, still exists. It was not an important event in itself, but for many years Sir Christopher had to work with this man who had a grudge against him, and it could not have been a pleasant thing for a mild and kindly man to have to bear.

Talman's spite might well have made mischief between Sir Christopher and his royal clients. It would not have been surprising if they had been alarmed at the thought of cracks large enough to take a man's finger appearing in their new home, but their faith in him was undiminished.

A new blow came, completely out of the blue, from Parliament, and it concerned St. Paul's, the building which of all others lay nearest to the architect's heart. Certain members of the St. Paul's commission considered—or pretended to consider—that the work on the great cathedral was going too slowly. For people who do not know a great deal about building, there always comes a time when the work seems to slow down. The outer walls go up, perhaps the roof goes on; the work is romping ahead; and then it all appears to decelerate and there is little new to see. People of experience know that this is a time of consolidation, of doing the thousand and one things which are essential, even if they do not show. In a house this phase may be a matter of weeks; in a great cathedral it is a matter of years.

Sir Christopher tried to explain the situation to his attackers, but with no success. They chose to believe that this upright and honorable man had deliberately slowed down the work in order to draw his salary for a longer period. Nothing could have been more offensive and damaging, and Sir Christopher was deeply hurt. The insult to his integrity was the worst part of this miserable affair. But as well as this, Sir Christopher had to submit to having his salary halved until the cathedral was finished—quite a serious financial blow. This was done, said the commissioners, "the better to encourage him to finish the same work with the utmost diligence and expedition."

A lesser man might quite justifiably have made a fuss. The accusation was so grossly unfair that it would have been possible to bring witnesses and to make out a very good case for the restoration of his full salary. Sir Christopher preferred to bear the insult in silence. He would not allow himself to be drawn into a public brawl. It was not until the cathedral was finished, in 1710, that he asked for what was owing to him, by then a large sum of money, and even then there was a great deal of unpleasantness, as we shall see later, before he got it.

In the meantime, there was other work to be done. The year before this attack upon his good faith, Sir Christopher had been commissioned by Queen Mary to build a hospital for retired seamen, on the same lines as Chelsea Hospital, on the site of the old Greenwich Palace.

Greenwich Palace had once stood on the banks of the Thames and had been the birthplace of Queen Elizabeth I. In the time of Charles I, the great architect Inigo Jones had been commissioned to build a new royal residence there, but civil war had rent the land in two before he could do more than build the Queen's House, which stood at some little distance inland. There was also another portion of a building on the riverbank, built at a later date from Inigo Jones's design, where Charles II had sometimes held court.

It was all a bit of a mess, but what was already there was good. The site was beautiful and, the Queen felt, appropriate for a seamen's home, being at the entrance to the port of London. It was not wanted by the King and Queen themselves; they had enough on their hands with Hampton Court and Kensington Palace and Whitehall. But it was a pity, the Queen thought, not to make use of what was already there. Sir Christopher Wren must use his ingenuity to link up the Queen's House and the other building and create something that would do honor both to London and to the Queen's philanthropic designs.

Nicholas Hawksmoor, writing about the subject many years later, said:

> Her Majesty Queen Mary, the foundress of the Marine Hospital, enjoined Sir Christopher Wren to build the Fabrick with great magnificence . . . and being ever solicitous for the prosecution of the design had several times honoured Greenwich with her personal views of the building erected by Charles II as part of his palace, and likewise of that built by Mr Inigo Jones, called the Queen's House . . . She was unwilling to demolish either, as was proposed by some. This occasioned the keeping of an approach from the Thames quite up to the Queen's House that Her Majesty might have access to that house by water as by land.

This determination of the Queen to keep the existing buildings intact posed a problem for Sir Christopher. It is usually easier to start a new project from scratch than to plan around what is already there, and in this case what was there was not even his own design. He had to plan his work to accord with the work of another man, and the fact that that man was the great Inigo Jones did not make it any easier. Moreover, as usual, the first plans he submitted were chopped and changed to suit the royal wishes. But Queen Mary never lived to see her benevolent scheme begun, let alone completed. On December 28, 1694, she died of smallpox, and Sir Christopher was thrown into a state of uncertainty and doubt. What would now happen to his plans for Greenwich? And would the King continue the rebuilding of Hampton Court? Sure enough, the work on the new palace was stopped and the army of workmen sent away. Sir Christopher had to console himself with the knowledge that part of St. Paul's was now open for services and the work, whatever his critics might say to the contrary, was going well. The choir was finished by the fall of 1697 and a service was held there on December 5, the first service in the cathedral since the fire. We can be sure that it was attended by Sir Christopher and his family. Young Christopher was then twenty-two. He had finished his time at Oxford in 1694 and was given the post of Clerk Engrosser at the Office of Works. He was a serious young man, devoted to his father and eager to follow in his footsteps and become an architect too.

The stopping of work on Hampton Court did at least give Sir Christopher more time to concentrate on Greenwich Hospital, which, fortunately, King William decided to complete. The work was finally begun in 1696. Then, two years later, fire once again took a hand in Sir Christopher's fortunes. A foreign maid, airing linen in the palace of Whitehall, so the story goes, hung the linen too close to the glowing coals in the grate and started a conflagration that destroyed a large part of the old buildings. We cannot imagine that this caused much grief to the asthmatic King William, who so much disliked Whitehall. It was an excellent excuse, he saw, to resume building at Hampton Court, and the word was given for full speed ahead. Joyfully Sir Christopher saw the army of workmen return and heard the ring of hammer on stone and the music of saws ripping through wood. He could not do all he wished to do, Hampton Court would never be a second Versailles, but it would be a fine palace just the same. Grinling Gibbons and Caius Gabriel Cibber were set to work to enrich the interior; landscape gardeners laid out the grounds. The sun shone on the rosy-red brick of the walls and sparkled on the blue summer waters of the Thames as it flowed quietly past on its way to the great port of London and the sea.

Whitehall obviously could not be left derelict. The Surveyor-General must draw up plans for its rebuilding, however reluctant the King might be to inhabit the palace. Perhaps a trifle wearily, Sir Christopher went back to the drawing board. He always seemed to be patching up Whitehall, and the recent fire had wiped out much of the work he had done on it at an earlier date. Still, there it was, in the heart of London. Many offices, such as his own Office of Works, were housed there, and the huge, damp, rambling complex of buildings, over which the smell of Thames mud hung like a pall, must be put in order.

Whitehall, Greenwich, Hampton Court, St. Paul's—Sir Christopher moved from one to another, attended by his devoted staff. Young Christopher was becoming a real help, and Nicholas Hawksmoor was obviously marked out for success. He was undertaking commissions for private houses on his own account and doing well. But Robert Hooke—poor, ailing Hooke—was no longer on the team. His health, always a preoccupation with him, finally broke down, and he retired. He died soon after the turn of the century, and all the members of the Royal Society attended the funeral of this brilliant man who had served them so well. Sir Christopher must have felt the loss keenly, for he and Hooke had been very close.

Sir Christopher was still receiving only half his salary for his work on St. Paul's, and he had undertaken the Greenwich Hospital work without a fee as his contribution to the charitable work the Seamen's Hospital would perform. It worried him a good deal that he had no real financial security. There was Jane, still unmarried, to be provided for; and William, in such poor health that any question of his earning a living had to be set aside. Talman was a thorn in his flesh. He was a man who could not be trusted and who was in a position to make more mischief if he wished. For the first time in his successful life, Sir Christopher allows a note of anxiety to creep into his letters.

Young Christopher had gone to France, on what we would now call a "working holiday." He was accompanied by one of the Strong family, a son of the master builder. The two young men were to combine enjoyment with the study of French architecture, just as Sir Christopher had done many years before. Young Christopher wanted to extend his tour to Italy, but his father wrote wistfully, asking for his return.

> I sent you to France at a time of business, as when you might make your observations and find acquaintance who

> might hereafter be useful to you in the future concernes of your life: if this be your ayme I willingly let you proceed provided you will soon returne, for these reasons; the little I have to leave you is unfortunately involved in trouble, and your presense would be a comfort to me, to assist me, not only for my sake, but your own that you might understand your affaires before it shall please God to take me from you, which, if suddenly, will leave you in perplexity and losse.

At that time, when a long life was the exception rather than the rule, Sir Christopher, nearly seventy, can be excused for bringing such pressure to bear on his son. How could he know, how could anyone know, that this frail little man who had never spared himself, who had done the work of ten men, had another twenty years to live?

Part V

THE DECLINING YEARS

Heroic Souls a nobler lustre find
Even from those griefs which break a vulgar mind;
That frost which cracks the brittle common glass,
Makes crystal into stronger brightness pass.

Dr. Sprat

15

The Storm Breaks

THE NEW CENTURY was ushered in by mild weather, a pleasant change from the hard frosts from which London had so frequently suffered in recent years. To have the Thames frozen over so hard that fairs could be held on it and oxen roasted whole might be fun to those citizens who had warm clothes and money to spend, but it was cruelly hard on the poor. The first January of the eighteenth century, however, was "like April for warmth and mildnesse," noted Evelyn in his diary.

It was easier to build in mild weather. Hard frost can bring work to a standstill; constant rain is a misery to those who labor out of doors; and high winds are a danger to men working at a height. Sir Christopher must have been heartened to see the progress that was being made on his various projects as the year advanced and the weather continued "warm, gentle and exceeding pleasant." St. Paul's grew rapidly. Even the commissioners should have been satisfied, although they still withheld half of Sir Christopher's salary. Greenwich Hospital took shape and promised to be an imposing landmark as London was approached by water. Hampton Court was nearly finished, and everyone was pleased with it.

But King William was not to enjoy his new palace in the peace of the countryside. He died in 1703 and his place was taken by Anne, the second daughter of James II and sister to Mary, who had been William's wife. Once again Sir Christopher, now a little weary, had to listen to the wishes of a new monarch and try to adapt the royal residences to suit still another royal taste.

The year after England saw a new queen on the throne was a year of personal sorrow for Sir Christopher Wren. His only daughter, Jane, his favorite child and loving companion, died. She was twenty-six and unmarried. Her father missed her very much. Now she was gone, and the big house in Scotland Yard was once again without a mistress. Sadly, Sir Christopher arranged for her burial in the still uncompleted St. Paul's, and commissioned Bird, one of the chief sculptors at work on the cathedral, to carve an elaborate monument showing Jane seated at an organ. The child he loved best should have her place in his best-loved building.

After Jane's death, and the loss of his close friend Robert Hooke, Sir Christopher began to feel the weight of his years, and was not sorry when a very able, youngish man called John Vanbrugh was appointed Comptroller of the Royal Works.

John Vanbrugh (later Sir John) was an outstanding figure of the time. His grandfather, Gillis van Brugg, had come to London from Ghent in Belgium in the time of

James I. His son, John's father, had worked as a "sugar baker," and at the time of the plague in 1665 had prudently removed himself and his family to Chester, in the northwest of England. There John went to school and from there he was sent to France to study the arts. He made good use of his time, and made a special study of architecture.

Not content with the studious life, he bought a commission in the army, and when he was twenty-six he ran into trouble. On the information of a rather mysterious lady, he was arrested as a spy at Calais and thrown into the Bastille. That he really was a spy is dubious, but it is a charge that is very hard to disprove, and for some time John fretted his heart out in captivity, with the future alarmingly uncertain. To take his mind off his troubles, he wrote a play, which he called *The Provok'd Wife*. Later, when he was, mercifully, released and rejoined his regiment, he polished up the play and promised himself that one day he would do something about it.

Home again a few years later, he visited the Theatre Royal, where a well-known actor, Colley Cibber, the son of Caius Cibber the sculptor, was acting in a play called *Love's Last Shift*.

"I could do better than that," we can imagine the versatile and confident young man telling himself, and he sat down to write a sequel to the play, using the same characters. In six weeks it was finished. He called it *The Relapse,* and presented it to Cibber, who recognized good work when he saw it. *The Relapse* was produced at the

Theatre Royal with Colley Cibber himself in the lead, and John Vanbrugh was launched as a playwright in London.

From the world of the theater to the world of architecture would seem to be a big step, but Vanbrugh took it without difficulty. No doubt he was helped by his social contacts. He "knew everybody," as the saying goes. His witty tongue and man-of-the-world manner made him popular in society. The influential Sir John Evelyn thought well of him, and he met men who had money and who wanted to improve their country homes. It was a great time for building. The old houses dating back to Elizabeth I were out of fashion. They were being torn down and Palladian mansions erected in their place, surrounded by carefully landscaped grounds. Vanbrugh was just the man to guide someone with more money than taste—and so he entered into his third profession. He had been a soldier and a playwright; now he was an architect as well, and soon attained an official post—Comptroller of the Royal Works.

Fortunately for Sir Christopher, who had to work with him, John Vanbrugh was what we would now call a Wren fan. He had his own very definite ideas, but he recognized Wren's genius. There could hardly have been a greater contrast than that between the aging Sir Christopher—a quiet, sober man of science, whose idea of amusement was an erudite discussion with friends over a bowl of chocolate in a coffeehouse—and the flamboyant playwright and man-of-the-world turned architect. All the same, the two men got on very well. Nicholas Hawksmoor made a third.

One wonders if young Christopher was ever jealous of these two men, nearer his own generation than his father's, who outshone him in every way. Perhaps he found comfort in his new home, for he was now a married man. His wife was the daughter of Phillip Musard, jeweler to Queen Anne, and soon he too had a son, whom he named Christopher, the fourth Christopher Wren in the family tree. It is to be hoped that the little grandson helped to comfort Sir Christopher for the loss of the daughter he had so dearly loved. There was now only one child left at home, the ailing William. Sir Christopher worried about William, so little able to face the world on his own, and he added a postscript to a letter sent to young Christopher in France, begging him to consider William his responsibility if the boy should be left alone.

The work of building went on all through the early years of the new century. St. Paul's was nearing completion. Greenwich Hospital, now largely under the direction of Vanbrugh, was taking shape. Blenheim Palace was built, with the help of Hawksmoor and Vanbrugh, and presented by a grateful country to the Duke of Marlborough, the great soldier and national hero. Vanbrugh was, in fact, the chosen architect for the palace—some say by the Duke's own wish—but Sir Christopher was there in the background to assist and advise. In this he showed again the sweetness of his nature. He might very well have expected, as he had a right to expect, that an official building such as a gift from the nation should be designed by the Surveyor-General, and to be passed over in favor of a new man, virtually unknown compared with himself, might well have been a blow to his pride and resented as such. If he did feel hurt, there is no record of it, and perhaps he was well out of it, for poor Vanbrugh spent years wrangling with the Duchess of Marlborough, who considered the whole place too large and inconvenient.

A smaller, though important work undertaken by the three men at about this time was an addition to Kensington Palace, an orangery for Queen Anne. This was used as a banqueting hall and was most charming, built of red brick, with numerous long windows reaching almost the full height of the front.

There was a great deal of trouble over this orangery, trouble with the contractors, and Vanbrugh wrote at length to the Lord Treasurer about the mismanagement. Perhaps Sir Christopher was not as careful as he should have been to keep an eye on all the people working under him. He was growing old, times were changing, new faces appeared, and it may well be that he was too trusting. Vanbrugh was careful, in his letter, not to make any personal charge against the man he loved and admired, but it is obvious Vanbrugh knew that Sir Christopher's inclination was to let things slide.

> He [Sir Christopher] always owned what I urged him to was right and often promised to join with me in overruling so bad a practice, but when I pressed him to the Execution he still evaded it, and that so many times, that at last I saw he never intended it and so I gave your Lordship the trouble of a complaint.

It was necessary to find another mason to work on the orangery—so much Vanbrugh got Sir Christopher to agree—and he even got from him the name of a man of whom he approved. But this was not the end of the trouble. Vanbrugh's letter goes on:

> He at last named one Hill, and gave me leave to send for him and give him Directions; which I presently did, and he promised me to go to Work. But a few days after, finding he had not begun, and enquiring into the reason; I found he had been frightened with some hints of what should befall him if he durst meddle with the Master Mason's business. And this had been so put home to him that he sent to me desire I would excuse him.

Poor Vanbrugh! Here he found himself up against something that employers are faced with today. The Master Masons was a guild. They had their rules, and unless you were a member of the guild they could make things very unpleasant for you. Hill was obviously not a member of the guild. This, however, was not the opinion of Sir Christopher Wren, who told the exasperated Vanbrugh that "the Man was a whimsical Man and a piece of an Astrologer and would venture upon nothing until he had consulted the Starrs, which probably he had not found favourably enclined upon this occasion and therefore had declined the work." "I desired he would employ somebody that was less superstitious which he said he would," the letter goes on. We can only sympathize with the frustrated John Vanbrugh and wonder, just a little, if Sir Christopher was not getting some fun out of seeing the younger man facing difficulties he had so often had to face himself.

Vanbrugh then went away for a short time on other business and returned to find a highly complicated situation, with one man doing the work but sending in his bills in another man's name, and all, apparently, with Sir Christopher's knowledge and consent. Vanbrugh writes, despairingly:

> This story is so very improbable, I'm afraid your Lordship will scarce give me credit for it, yet it is a plain and literal truth in every Article. As for Sir Chris. Wren I don't believe he has any interest in his part of it; but your Lordship will see by this Decisive proof the power these Fellows have over him which they never made so effectual a use of as when they prevailed with him . . . to let 'em have a Clerk of the Works of Whitehall . . . one who by nature is a very poor Wretch; and by a many years course of morning Drunkenness, has made himself a dos'd Sott.

Perhaps Sir Christopher was too easygoing with the contractors. It would be quite out of keeping with his character if he were a fierce man of business, watching every penny. On the other hand, Vanbrugh was new to the job; he may not have realized that the contractors were often owed a great deal of money by the government, or by the monarch, and when money is owing, it is not always possible or wise to take a high hand.

In 1708 came a new task for the aging Surveyor-General. Fifty new parish churches were to be built for the rapidly growing population of London. Sir Christopher knew that he would have to delegate most of the work to Hawksmoor and Vanbrugh, but his experience of church building was there to help them, and he gave a great deal of thought to the whole concept.

The first thing he urged the authorities to consider was the location of these new churches. They must be built where they were most needed. Land was cheaper in the suburbs, but it would be money well spent to buy plots in the crowded parts of the town, convenient for the people the churches were meant to serve. And if they followed his advice, the plots need not be large, for he considered that the custom of having people buried in the church and a graveyard around the building was a great mistake.

> I could wish all Burials in Churches might be disallowed which is not only unwholesome, but the Pavements can never be kept even nor Pews upright. And if the Church-yard be close around the Church this also is inconvenient, because the ground being continually raised by the Graves, occasions, in Time, a Descent by Steps into the Church, which renders it damp, and the Walls green, as appears evidently in all old Churches.

The solution, he felt, was obvious, and so it would seem to us, although it was a new and revolutionary idea at the time. They must have cemeteries on the outskirts of the town, and these could be made very pleasant, with a brick wall around them, and yew trees and paths where people could walk. Memorials (carefully regulated by an architect) for the dead, and good air and walks for the living, was what these cemeteries would provide, and if they were bordered by fields, "they will bound the excessive

Growth of the City with a graceful border." Sir Christopher envisaged what today we call the "green belt."

The old man—now seventy-six—sat long at his desk working out in every detail how these new churches should be built. He considered the site, which he urged should be in a wide street where the carriages of the rich would not create a traffic block. He went into the question of bells, and of the materials the churches should be built of. London bricks, he considered, were as good as you could get, *if,* and it was a big if, they were properly made. In the great demand for materials in that age of building, the price had risen and the quality fallen. Bricks were only too often badly mixed and "half-baked" and in consequence would not bear any great weight. The best stone was Portland stone, which had proved its worth over the years, and the best kind of lime cockleshell lime, which, well beaten with sand, made the strongest mortar. Good oak for the roof, "because it will bear some neglect." Speaking from bitter experience, he says, "The Church-Wardens care may be defective in speedy mending Drips; they usually white-wash the Church and set up their Names, but neglect to preserve the Roof over their heads."

Next he considers the size of the churches, which would have to hold at least two thousand people each to cope with the demand of an expanding population. At the same time, everybody must be able to see and hear, so that they could take part in the service. And since everyone must

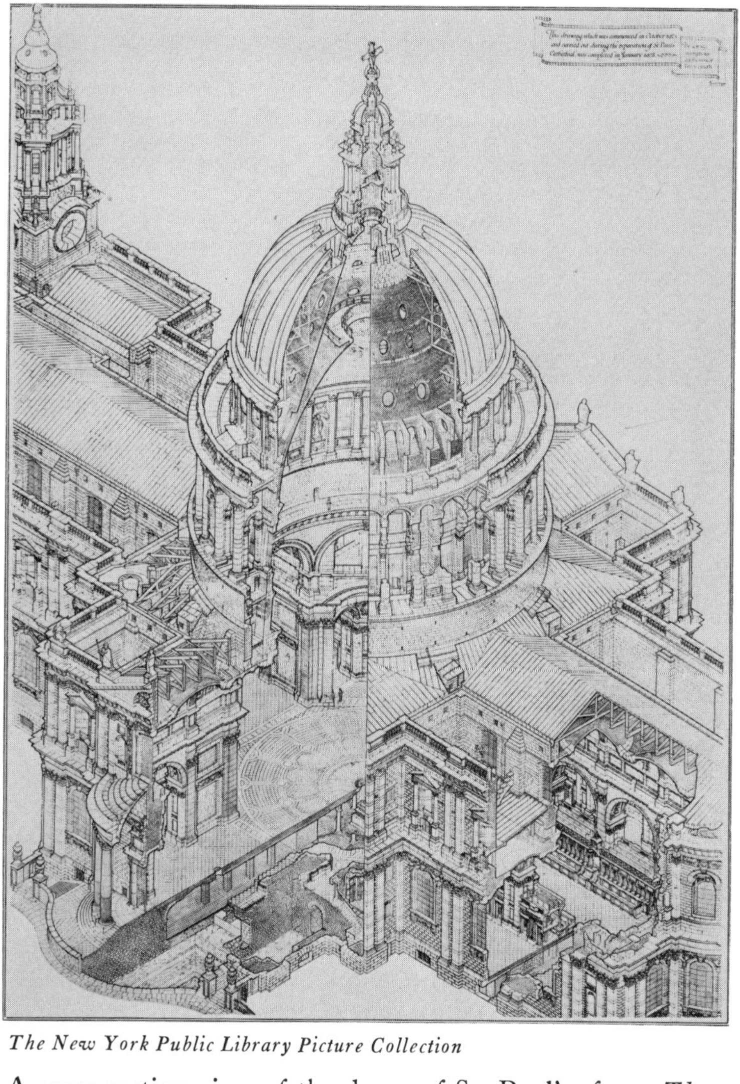

The New York Public Library Picture Collection

A cross-section view of the dome of St. Paul's, from *The Illustrated London News*

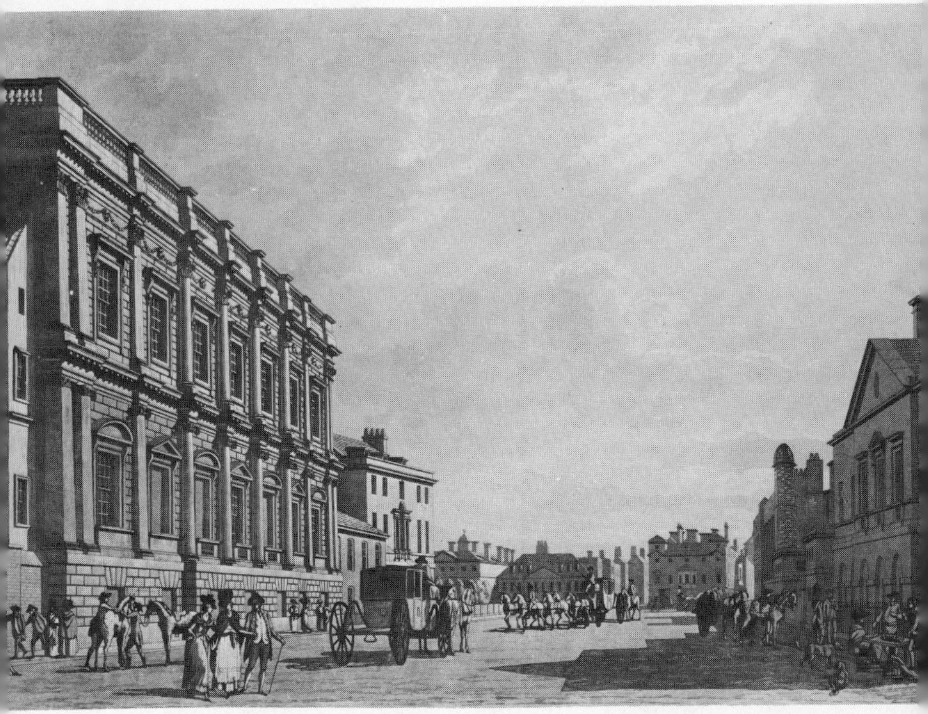

Courtesy The Guildhall Library, London

A view showing Sir Christopher Wren's additions to Whitehall Palace

Courtesy The Guildhall Library, London

A contemporary view of Kensington Palace

The New York Public Library Picture Collection

The exterior of St. Paul's

Courtesy The Guildhall Library, London

The choir of St. Paul's

Courtesy The Guildhall Library, London

Greenwich Hospital

"The Thames from Somerset House Terrace towards the City," a painting by Canaletto showing St. Paul's Cathedral. *Copyright reserved*

Courtesy The Guildhall Library, London

Hampton Court Palace

hear the sermon, the placing of the pulpit would be of the greatest importance.

> A moderate voice may be heard 50 feet distant before the Preacher, 30 feet on each side and 20 behind the Pulpit, and not this unless the Pronunciation be distinct and equal without losing the Voice at the last Word of the Sentence which is commonly emphatical and if obscured spoils the whole sense . . . I mention this as an insufferable fault in the Pronunciation of some of our otherwise excellent Preachers; which schoolmasters might correct in the young.

Such excellent advice, and needed as badly now as it was when Sir Christopher Wren laid down his quill.

16

Dismissed

IT WAS A GREAT MOMENT for the architect and everyone else connected with the cathedral when young Christopher and his friend Strong, the mason, laid the last stone upon the lantern over the dome of St. Paul's. This occurred shortly after the day when Queen Anne, "full of jewels," as a contemporary account tells us, paid a state visit to celebrate a great military victory on September 7, 1704. The interior of the cathedral, just finished, was dazzling in its new beauty and grandeur. The white Portland stone, still unsullied by London soot, shone like snow against the late-summer blue of the sky; marble glowed softly under the sun's rays; gilding caught and held the light. The carvings of Gibbons, Cibber, Bird, and many others were picked out and intensified by the glow of a great host of candles. The cathedral had come alive.

It should have been a time of triumph for Sir Christopher, the culmination of thirty-five years of work. Unfortunately, it was marred by bitterness and quarreling, which dragged on and on.

On a chilly day in February 1710, Sir Christopher sat down with a heavy heart to write a letter to the Queen.

He begged her to use her authority with the commissioners so that he might be allowed to finish St. Paul's in his own way and without the continual petty interference to which he was being subjected. He pointed out that his salary had been halved until the building was complete, but that it never would be complete unless he was left alone and allowed to get on with the work as he thought fit. He then waited, hopefully, for conditions to improve.

It was the end of April before his letter was brought to the attention of the commissioners, and for all the good it did him, he might have spared himself the trouble of writing it. The commissioners issued a report full of unpleasant hints about Wren's honesty and competence. They were careful not to make any plain accusations, which might have got them into trouble, but the insinuations were there. Sir Christopher, they hinted, if not corrupt himself, had at least turned a blind eye on the corruption of his subordinates. They denied that they were responsible for stopping half of his salary; it was Parliament, they said, who had done that. All they were concerned with was to "hasten the finishing of the work."

The report then went into great detail about an iron fence over which there had been a conflict of opinion with the architect. The commissioners claimed that Sir Christopher had put up "a poor mean rail disliked by everyone," while Jennings, a master carpenter and one of Sir Christopher's most trusted men, had, they said, sold the iron provided for a better fence, and much else besides, and they asked that Jennings might be prosecuted for theft.

It was all very worrying for an old man. Perhaps he had been a little careless with his workmen. Perhaps they were taking advantage of his age to feather their own nests. And yet—they were good men, old and tried friends. Was he now to confront them with charges of dishonesty?

It was a wretched situation. For so many years he had lived at peace with everyone. And now, when old age was an enemy which could not be held at bay much longer, he had also to fight ill will, suspicion, and unfair treatment. The frail old man must have felt very much alone as he sat at his desk to write yet more letters, to try at least to get what was his due.

> *To His Grace the Archbishop of Canterbury and the Bishop of London.*
>
> May it please your Lordships that I humbly lay before you the state of the suspension of a moiety of my salary . . .
>
> *To the Honourable the Commons of Great Britain in Parliament assembled.*
>
> The humble petition of Sir Christopher Wren . . . That your petitioner having been surveyor of the said Cathedral church from the beginning of its rebuilding and the same (as may be seen) being now completed, excepting the iron fence, some ornaments undetermined, and some other matters which some of the commissioners for the fabric have so interposed in, as that his measures for completing the same are wholely overruled and frustrated and thereby he is under this hardship as neither to be paid the salary that is due to him, nor suffered to perfect the work that is made the condition of it.
>
> Your petitioner, therefore, most humbly prays your

honours to grant him such relief in the premises as to your great wisdom and justice shall seem meet.

The great wisdom and justice of the House of Commons may sometimes be questioned, but in this case they did the right thing. Sir Christopher at long last received what he was owed, a substantial sum of money.

This was satisfactory, but there was more trouble to come. Two years later a pamphlet appeared—its title, "Frauds and Abuses at St Paul's," and its subtitle, "Letter to a Member of Parliament."

Sir Christopher read this pamphlet with a sinking of the heart. That he should have made enemies in the course of his long and brilliant career was unavoidable, but that anyone should feel such personal spite against him must have caused him great distress.

This "letter" was supposed to be written in the interests of a parish church called St. Mary Woolnoth, which had asked that the cost of rebuilding the church should be paid out of the surplus money left over from St. Paul's. They had been refused. This was reasonable enough. If there was any money left over from the actual building of the cathedral, it was needed for internal fitments and other necessities of a cathedral church. But the letter ignored this and claimed that if the cathedral was not complete, "it was the fault of Persons belonging to it."

Worse was to come. Sir Christopher Wren was mentioned by name and accused of dishonesty. The business of the iron fence was raked up again, and so was the case of

Jennings the carpenter, who was said to have been dismissed for stealing and reinstated in a highhanded manner by Sir Christopher Wren.

Sir Christopher might have disregarded the attacks upon himself, but the slur on the faithful Jennings was too much for him to bear in silence. He seized his pen and wrote a complete reply to all the charges, which he published together with a detailed statement of the accounts relating to St. Paul's building fund. But if he had enemies, he also had friends. Before his letter appeared, a tract was published entitled "Facts against Scandal," which was wholeheartedly on Sir Christopher's side.

Battle was now joined. The unknown enemy struck again with a pamphlet bearing the unwieldy title "A Continuation of Frauds and Abuses at St Paul's." No sooner had this appeared than Wren's anonymous defender countered with a second part of "Facts against Scandal," and this time he made such mincemeat of all the accusations that the enemy was defeated and was heard no more.

For a short while Sir Christopher was left in peace, and was able to give his mind to family affairs. Young Christopher, like his father, lost his first wife after only a short period of marriage and, again like his father, was left with a baby boy. In 1715 he married again, the widow of a Warwickshire gentleman, Sir Roger Burgoyne. Warwickshire is a most beautiful county in the very heart of England, and here Sir Christopher bought for his son an estate called Wroxall Abbey, where young Christopher settled down to be a country squire, although he still retained his post as Clerk Engrosser at the Office of Works. A second son, Stephen, was born, and it was Stephen who, in years to come, published the Wren family history that his father had put together. In it the story is told of Dr. Wren, Dean of Windsor; Matthew Wren, Bishop of Ely; and Sir Christopher Wren, architect and man of science. Stephen could not have remembered his famous grandfather very well, since he would have been about six or seven when the great man died. But his elder brother, Kit, would have known him better.

WITH THE COMPLETION OF ST. PAUL'S IN 1711, Sir Christopher, now seventy-nine, might well have felt he was entitled to retire, to leave the quarrelsome, scrambling world behind him, to let others take up his burden. But the indomitable old man was not yet ready to rest. Although he was prepared to delegate duties to the talented men of his team, especially John Vanbrugh, he still could not bring himself to leave the work he loved so well. He did, however, spend less time in his office, where young Christopher had quietly taken over many of the routine tasks. And he left the great house in Scotland Yard and moved to a small house at Hampton Court Green which he rented from the Crown. He also had rooms in St. James's Street near the Office of Works, and he drove from one to the other in his own coach, enjoying equally the company and good talk he could command in town and the pure air and quiet of the countryside. His staff, who had a warm affection for him, tried to see that he did not do too much—physically, at any rate. No one could control his active brain.

In 1714 Queen Anne died, George I came to the throne, and with his coming began the decline of Sir Christopher Wren. Perhaps he sometimes, sadly and wearily, considered himself to be like a guest who, loved and honored, is nevertheless beginning to outstay his welcome. He had seen, not one, but two generations of men rising up to take his place. Vanbrugh and Hawksmoor themselves were now middle-aged, and to the men who were pushing forward, Wren seemed very much behind the times. Now, surely, would have been the moment to retire, to bow out gracefully, leaving the stone jungle of the great city and the intrigues of ambitious men for a quiet seat by the river Thames, for leisurely reading and musing over memories of past triumphs. With hindsight, we can see that this would have been the wise thing to do. But Sir Christopher thought otherwise. He stayed on at his post and saw great changes take place all around him. The whole constitution of the Office of Works was revised and a board was formed to carry out the duties of Surveyor, the duties which for nearly fifty years had been his alone. True, he was a member of the Board, together with Vanbrugh, who received a knighthood, and others, but he was no longer the King's Surveyor-General. He was allowed to keep his title of Surveyor, but it was now an empty thing, and he had no special powers.

It was the beginning of the end. In the following year

Sir Christopher reluctantly gave up the surveyorship of Greenwich Hospital to Vanbrugh, and on April 26, 1718, the final blow fell. Sir Christopher Wren, then eighty-six, was deprived even of the empty title of Surveyor-General of the Royal Works, to be succeeded by William Benson, a favorite of the new king. Benson had little experience as an architect, so in a way history repeated itself, since Sir Christopher himself, the astronomer and mathematician, had been appointed over the heads of more highly qualified men by his patron, Charles II. In this case, however, the royal hunch was not successful. Benson was hopelessly incompetent, and after having disorganized the whole Office of Works and got rid of some good men, including Hawksmoor, he was himself dismissed in disgrace, after having made a hash of repairs to the House of Lords.

During Benson's short tenure at the Office of Works, he managed to stir up trouble for Sir Christopher and the rest of the Board, accusing them of mismanagement. By now the old man was living quietly at Hampton Court, but he could not allow his reputation and that of his friends on the Board to be sullied in this way. He dictated a letter to the Lords of the Treasury which he signed, shakily, in his own hand. The letter is as clear and vigorous as any he wrote in his life. The charges were false, he wrote. The Board had been composed of men of integrity and it was shameful that this upstart, Benson, should accuse them of dishonest practice. In the last years of his working life he had had more than enough of sly innuendoes and dark hints of sharp practice. Mild and tolerant man though he was, he would not submit quietly to any more, and he trusted that this last attack would be the end. His letter concludes:

> . . . having worn out (by God's Mercy) a long life in the Royal Service, and having made some Figure in the World, I hope it will be allowed me to Die in Peace.
>
> *I am, may it please yr Ldships,*
> *With most sincere Respect,*
> *Yr Ldships most Obedient Humble Servant,*
>
> CHR. WREN.

But the long life was not yet quite worn out. Christopher Wren still had five more years to live.

17

Gently, to the End

THE RIVER THAMES flows gently past Hampton Court Palace, and in the spring the gardens are full of daffodils, and the horse chestnuts hold out their pink and white candles of blossom. Here, in the house on Hampton Court Green, the venerable Sir Christopher Wren settled down quietly to wait for his allotted time to end. But he did not wait in idleness. He still retained one official position; he was Director of Works of Westminster Abbey, and for many years he had been gradually getting the fabric of the great church into repair, assisted by a number of his faithful team. It was to keep an eye on the abbey that the old man, every so often, drove up to London to stay at his rooms in St. James's Street. No doubt he took advantage of these visits to see old friends, although there were now very many gaps in the ranks. Sir John Evelyn had been dead for some years, and Samuel Pepys even longer. Hooke was gone, Cousin Matthew Wren was gone, and Whitehall was swarming with Germans brought over by George I. There were strange faces everywhere, and new ways. Sir Christopher must often have felt, sadly, that he had outlived his time.

But if colleagues died, at least the thirst for knowledge lived on within him. The problem of longitude at sea, which he and Robert Hooke had worked on together, was still unsolved, and he bent his mind to this once again, writing a memorandum about it in cipher. He kept himself occupied and he was contented. Perhaps young Christopher brought his little sons to visit their famous grandfather in his country retreat. It may well be that Stephen was drawing on childhood memories as well as on hearsay when, many years later, he wrote in *Parentalia:*

> He betook himself to a country retreat . . . in which Recess, free from worldly Affairs he passed the greatest part of the five last following years of his Life in Contemplation and Studies and principally in the Consolation of the holy scriptures: cheerful in Solitude, and as well pleased to die in the Shade as in the Light.

In 1720, one last attempt was made to discredit the great man's work. A rumor was started that the roof of the Sheldonian Theatre, on which Sir Christopher had spent so much thought and ingenuity, was unsafe and in danger of collapse. The architect himself was now too feeble to journey all the way to Oxford to inspect and report, but a committee of experts was formed who very soon categorically pronounced the roof to be in "perfect order and good repair." If the rumor had been started in spite, then the unknown enemy was confounded, and Sir Christopher's mind put at rest, if indeed it had ever been disturbed. For the rare ability to keep calm, to refuse to allow himself to be "fussed," is most certainly what kept

Sir Christopher Wren going through his long and busy life. He had the knack of detaching himself from everything except the thing he was working on at the time. He had perfect powers of concentration—and this in itself made him seem, at times, a little remote, even unfeeling, although this was far from being the case. It was this calmness, coupled with excellent common sense, which kept him healthy, though he was never robust.

Stephen writes:

> As to his bodily constitution it was naturally more delicate than strong especially in his youth, which seemed consumptive; and yet by a judicious Regularity and Temperance (having acquired good knowledge in Physick) he continued healthy, with little Intermission even to this extreme old Age. Further 'tis observable, that he was happily endued with such an Evenness of Temper, a steady Tranquility of Mind and Christian Fortitude, that no injurious Incidents, or Inquietudes of human life could ever ruffle or discompose.

Once every year, during that quiet time at Hampton Court, it was Sir Christopher's custom to drive up to St. Paul's Cathedral and sit for a while in the great space under the dome. Perhaps he spent the time in prayer, perhaps he just let his mind wander back through the years while the peace and beauty of his creation brought him happiness and a sense of fulfillment. It would have been wiser, perhaps, for an old man to have made his pilgrimage in the summer. But in February 1723 he may have known he had not long to live and if he wanted to see his masterpiece once again, there was no time to be lost.

He drove to London through the bitter cold, kept his vigil in the chill of the great church, and drove home again to warmth and comfort, which came too late. He felt chilled to the bone, but he dined, as he always did, in the bow-windowed, ground-floor room looking out onto the Green. After dinner, again as usual, he slept in his chair by the fire. He slept longer than he was in the habit of doing, and at last his manservant, feeling worried, tapped gently and went into the silent room. There he found a great emptiness, for Sir Christopher Wren, his face calm and peaceful, was dead.

He is buried in the crypt of St. Paul's Cathedral, and on his monument are carved the words: SI MONUMENTUM REQUIRIS CIRCUMSPICE: "If you seek his monument, look around."

Chronological Table

1632	Birth of Christopher Wren
1642	Went to Westminster School
1646	Left school. Worked with Sir Charles Scarborough
1649	Wadham College, Oxford
1651	Graduated B.A.
1657	Appointed Professor of Astronomy, Gresham College, London
1660	Restoration of the monarchy Foundation of the Royal Society
1661	Appointed Savillian Professor of Astronomy at Oxford
1663	Model of Sheldonian Theatre shown to Royal Society
1665	Paris visit. The plague strikes London
1666	Great Fire of London
1669	Appointed Surveyor-General
1670	City churches begun
1673	St. Paul's, the "Great Model"
1675	St. Paul's, the "Warrent design" accepted
1676	Trinity College (Cambridge) Library begun
1682	Chelsea Hospital begun
1689	Hampton Court and Kensington Palaces begun

1696	Greenwich Hospital begun
1697	St. Paul's choir finished. Dome begun
1711	St. Paul's officially complete
1718	Wren dismissed from Surveyorship
1723	Death of Sir Christopher Wren

A Catalogue of New Theories, Inventions, Experiments and Mechanic Improvements

exhibited by Mr Wren at the first Assemblies at Wadham College in Oxford, for Advancement of Natural and Experimental Knowledge, called then the New Philosophy: Some of which, on the Return of publick Tranquility, were improved and perfected, and with other useful Discoveries, communicated to the Royal Society

Picture of the Pleiades
New facile exact Ways of Observation
To find whether the Earth moves
The Weather-Wheel
Weather Clock
Perpetual Motion or weather-wheel and weather clock compounded
The Ballance, to weigh without Weights
Strainer of the Breath, to make the same air serve in Respiration
Artificial Eye with the Humours truly and dioptically made
To write in the Dark
To write double by an instrument
Several new Ways of graving and etching
To weave many Ribbons at once with only turning a Wheel
Divers Improvements in the Art of Husbandry
Divers new Engines for raising of Water

A pavement, harder, fairer and cheaper than Marble
To grind Glasses
A Way of Imbroidery for Beds, Hangings, cheap and fair
New Ways of Printing
Pneumatick Engines
New Designs tending to Strength, Convenience and Beauty in Building
Divers new Musical Instruments
A Speaking Organ, articulating Sounds
New Ways of Sailing
The Best ways for reckoning Time, Way, Longitude and observing at Sea
Probable Ways for making fresh Water at Sea
To stay long under Water
Ways of submarine Navigation
Easier ways of Whale-fishing
New Ways of Intelligence, new Cyphers
Some Inventions in Fortification
To pierce a Rock in Mineing
Some Anatomical Experiments
To Measure the Basis and Height of a Mountain, only by journeying over it
To Measure the straight distance by travelling the winding Way
A Compass to play in a Coach, or the Hand of the Rider
To perfect Coaches for Ease, Strength and Lightness etc.

Sources

Parentalia	STEPHEN WREN
The Diary of John Evelyn	
The Diary of Samuel Pepys	
The Diary of Robert Hooke	
English Social History	G. M. TREVELYAN
King Charles II	ARTHUR BRYANT
A Brief History of the Royal Society	ANDRADE
The Architecture of Sir Christopher Wren	VIKTOR FURST
The Age of Wren	RALPH DUTTON
Wren	GEOFFRY WEBB
Sir Christopher Wren	LENA MILMAN
Sir Christopher Wren	JOHN SUMMERSON
Samuel Pepys, the Man in the Making	ARTHUR BRYANT
The Plague and the Fire	JAMES LEASOR
London Masons of the 17th Century	KNOOP AND JONES

Index

Rosemary Weir

The Man Who Built a City

A LIFE OF SIR CHRISTOPHER WREN

Just before midnight on September 1, 1666, a fire began that in four days' time virtually leveled the City of London, the mile-square walled enclave that had existed since Roman times and is part of the London we know today. The talented man who would design and rebuild it was already on the scene. Inventor at the age of fifteen, professor of astronomy at twenty-five, brilliant mathematician, Sir Christopher Wren now turned as successfully to architecture. Throughout London and beyond, the beautiful "Wren buildings" still stand.

Numerous and far-ranging as Wren's accomplishments were, he is known today primarily as the man who rebuilt St. Paul's Cathedral—the